THE JESUS YOU NEED TO KNOW

A Character Study
of the Christ

JOE DURSO

WESTBOW
PRESS®
A DIVISION OF THOMAS NELSON
& ZONDERVAN

Scripture quotations marked NASB are taken from the New American Standard Bible©, Copyright © 1960, 1962, 1963, 1968, 1971, 1972, 1973, 1975, 1977, 1995 byThe Lockman Foundation. Used by permission.

NET Bible® copyright ©1996-2006 by Biblical Studies Press, L.L.C. http://netbible.com All rights reserved.

WestBow Press books may be ordered through booksellers or by contacting:

WestBow Press
A Division of Thomas Nelson & Zondervan
1663 Liberty Drive
Bloomington, IN 47403
www.westbowpress.com
1 (866) 928-1240

ISBN: 978-1-5127-6507-6 (sc)
ISBN: 978-1-5127-6508-3 (hc)
ISBN: 978-1-5127-6506-9 (e)

Library of Congress Control Number: 2016919427

Print information available on the last page.

WestBow Press rev. date: 5/30/2017

To my Lord and Savior Jesus Christ, who alone is worthy of all honor, praise, and glory, and without whom I would have no reason to write this book.

"And this is eternal life, that they might know You, the only true God, and Jesus Christ whom You have sent." (John 17:3)

"Jesus said to him, "Have I been so long with you, and yet you have not come to know Me, Philip?" (John 14:9a)

"More than that, I count all things to be loss in view of the surpassing value of knowing Christ Jesus my Lord, for whom I have suffered the loss of all things, and count them but rubbish so that I may gain Christ." (Philippians 3:8)

"Grace and peace be multiplied to you in the knowledge of God and of Jesus our Lord; seeing that His divine power has granted to us everything pertaining to life and godliness, through the true knowledge of Him who called us by His own glory and excellence." (2 Peter 1:2–3)

CONTENTS

PREFACE

Often after proclaiming the gospel to others, I have desired to place something in their hands along with the scriptures: a detailed description of the Jesus of the Bible. Nothing is more important than for a person to see Jesus. Whether Jew, Muslim, atheist, Buddhist, or Catholic, all need to see Jesus as the One they need more than all others. The gospel is the good news that Jesus came into the world to save men from their sins, and this book is meant expressly to shed more light on the person of Jesus—His character, motives, integrity, honor, and glory. In human history there is no person who came before Jesus, and no one who will ever come after Him, who will in any way measure up to Him, because He is the one true and living God in human flesh.

It is possible to know Jesus only from the pages of scripture, because it alone is the authoritative, infallible, and inerrant Word of God. The Bible proclaims itself to be "sharper than any two edged sword, piercing to the dividing asunder of soul and spirit, even to the joint and marrow of the bone, and is a discerner of both the thoughts and intentions of the heart" (Hebrews 4:12). The Bible that reveals to men intimate things about themselves is the same book that reveals Jesus in intricate detail and panoramic splendor. It is from the pages of scripture that men should see Jesus, according to what God has said and not what false teachers have misconstrued about Him.

In seeing the Jesus of the Bible, we see the truth about the world, sinners, and saints. Only in seeing Jesus can we understand what God intended all men to become, according to the plan He set in motion, and by the only means available to accomplish the unthinkable. The means God used to accomplish the unthinkable is Himself in the person of His Son, the Lord Jesus Christ. The unthinkable task that He alone accomplishes is to change hopelessly wicked and damned sinners into pure and holy saints destined for glory with Him.

The true and unaltered gospel of Jesus Christ proclaims Jesus of Nazareth to be the one true Savior of men, and it can only be rightfully understood through an accurate knowledge of Him. To understand Jesus, His correct message must be received and then experienced through rebirth, which alone can reunite a sinner with God, who does not tolerate sinful men. Only a true knowledge of Jesus can inform blinded sinners of their wicked condition before the holiness of God. It is only the light of Jesus that properly unveils our true condition and reveals how far short we all fall from meriting God's favor.

It is my hope that in the pages of this book you will come to know the Jesus who can save your soul. I do not mean that you merely understand facts about Him but that you come to know Him personally as you know your closest friend or relative. To know Jesus is to know the one person who knows you better than you know yourself, the only person who has the power to forgive your sins and to love you with a love that is unconditional and completely satisfying.

ACKNOWLEDGMENTS

To everyone who has reflected Jesus to me in one form or another: I love you all, with thanks and appreciation.

To my wife, whose unselfishness allowed me all the time necessary to prepare this book's manuscript: her selfless service to others has caused me to see my own selfishness, the cross, and Jesus.

To my son, Paul, whose moral integrity, pursuit of accountability, and repentant heart help me to see what Jesus can accomplish in a believer.

To all the men and women who took the time to contribute to my spiritual growth during the 49 years leading up to the writing and completion of this book.

To all my brothers and sisters in Christ, through whom God has revealed to me the Jesus of whom this book speaks.

To all the men and women who contributed by prayer, financial support, and encouragement through all my feelings of inadequacy while writing *The Jesus You Need to Know*.

INTRODUCTION

This book follows the life of Christ in a logical sequence of events. First, we observe the preexistent Jesus, who is eternal God and creator of all things. Next, we discuss Jesus's early childhood, followed by the years of His ministry leading up to His death and resurrection. After that, we consider Jesus' high-priestly office, followed by His coming kingdom and the consummation of all things. Some chapters, such as "Jesus Does All Things Well" and "Jesus' Defining Union" are not part of His human timeline.

The subtitle of this book is "A Character Study of the Christ," because the focus of the book is the moral integrity and characteristics of Jesus Christ. The Christian message is the gospel of Jesus Christ, which is the good news that Jesus Christ came to fulfill God the Father's plan to save men from their sins. The greatest motivation to receive the message of Jesus is Jesus Himself. His moral integrity and trustworthiness draw men to Him. This present world system, which directs people where they naturally want to go, is characterized by desire to rise to the top, to be left alone, or to do good deeds without a love for the one true God. Jesus perfectly introduced a form of life that makes love the most desirable thing on earth. The life that Jesus lived flowed from a heart filled with an uncompromising love for God and His fellow man. It is Jesus's heart—His motives, attitudes, desire, and will—that make Him the most desirable person in the universe. It is the desirable person of Jesus whom the author has attempted to describe publicly and accurately.

The content of this book is not only about what Jesus did—His death on the cross, the promises He made and fulfilled, or even the promises made about Him that were fulfilled—but about why He gave Himself so sacrificially and lovingly to God and men. The Bible is the only book in the world that goes so deeply into the hearts of men to reveal our motives, and so it is that it reveals the very heart of God in the person of Jesus Christ. It is not sufficient or prudent to go through life as a mindless animal, because God did not create man to live life that way. The animal kingdom reveals to us life without laws or conscience, but men are different.

Men were not meant to work, play, and reproduce without understanding that there is a greater and higher purpose behind it all. It is my purpose to show that Jesus properly revealed that higher purpose by exposing false religions through His teaching and by elevating man to God's transcendent purpose through the life He lived. Christ's moral purity and unparalleled integrity unveil evil in the world. His death and resurrection deliver men who believe in Him from the consequences of their evil choices. God's love is unrivaled as it is revealed in Christ. However, His patience toward the wickedness of men is not eternal. At the end of human history, His wrath on sin will be revealed just before the terrible Day of the Lord known as the White Throne Judgment.

The overarching purpose in writing this book is to give the reader the best reason in the world to receive Jesus's message—through the life He lived, and the heart, character, and integrity it took to live it.

WITHIN GOD IS A HEART OF INTIMACY

"And this is eternal life, that they might know you, the only true God, and Jesus Christ whom you have sent." John 17:3

"Jesus said to him, "Have I been so long with you, and yet you have not come to know Me, Philip?" John 14:9

"More than that, I count all things to be loss in view of the surpassing value of knowing Christ Jesus my Lord, for whom I have suffered the loss of all things, and count them but rubbish so that I may gain Christ," (Philippians 3:8)

"Grace and peace be multiplied to you in the knowledge of God and of Jesus our Lord; seeing that His divine power has granted to us everything pertaining to life and godliness, through the true knowledge of Him who called us by His own glory and excellence." (2 Peter 1:2, 3)

Intimacy:
"Into Me You See"

CHAPTER 1

THE JESUS YOU NEED TO KNOW: THE DESIRABLE CHARACTER OF GOD'S LOVE

Have you ever asked yourself, "If there's a God, why hasn't He made Himself known to me?"? In reality, God made Himself known when He endowed humans with reason, by which we all ask the question: where did everything come from?

Reason is based on cause and effect. Where there's an effect, there's a cause. Therefore, we see a house and ask, "Who built it?"

When we inquire about the origin of the universe, we're faced with two basic options: God or evolution. Self-creation is against reason, because in order to create yourself, you would have to exist before you existed. It takes faith to believe in an eternal, self-existent God, but not as much faith as it takes to believe in a universe without Him.

The only answer to a universe that's as large and complex as ours is a God who is eternal and infinite, which brings us to the purpose of this book. It has the same purpose as the Gospel according to John, where we read, "Therefore many other signs Jesus also performed in the presence of the disciples, which are not written in this book; but these have been written so that you may believe that Jesus is the Christ, the Son of God; and that believing you may have life in His name" (John 20:30–31).

The focus of this book is Jesus, the one who imparts eternal life and the faith that is necessary for salvation.

There's natural faith, and there's saving faith. Saving faith is as much a gift as is Jesus Christ. It takes the right kind of faith to be saved, just as it takes faith in the right Jesus. The apostle James once wrote, "You believe that God is one. You do well; the demons also believe, and shudder" (James 2:19).

At a time when evolution rules, it's difficult to believe in God. Belief in just any god is not enough to rescue a person from the one true God's righteous anger, which results from our sins. Apart from the Word of God, every one of Adam's race believes himself or herself to be good, which is what makes judgment upon sinners so hard to accept. It takes saving faith in the Jesus of the Bible in order for a person to be saved.

The right kind of faith is always accompanied by repentance, because faith takes God at His word. Repentance is the turning from sin after a person acknowledges that he or she is sinful. God's Word makes it perfectly clear that all sin and are worthy of His punishment (Romans 3:23).

The people who read the Bible and say they don't sin enough for punishment call God a liar. The person who possesses saving faith doesn't call God a liar (1 John 1:10). Furthermore, saving faith is defined by the apostle John in his gospel: "But as many as received Him, to them He gave the right to become children of God, even to those who believe in His name" (John 1:12).

According to John saving faith is to receive Christ and "receive" in the Greek, means "to give a person access to oneself and to make one's own; .these are terms of relationship, commitment, devotion, and trust.

People who exercise saving faith first accept God's indictments against them, and then they trust God to keep His promises to save through Christ and with full commitment to His rule. Even if a person accepts the fact that he or she is sinful, there remains this question: why should anyone believe that Jesus saves? You should believe that Jesus saves, because the most unique book in the entire world declares Jesus Christ to be the only savior.

The Bible took 1,200 years to write, and it was written by more than forty human authors, in three different languages, with one central and unified theme. The Bible contains hundreds of specific prophecies about the coming Savior, all of which are fulfilled in Christ. The Bible is the only book to be written by men with the audacity to say, "Thus says the Lord."

The Bible is also the only book that proves itself to be inspired by God by virtue of its integrity, prophetic content, honesty, and heart-piercing truth. You should believe that Jesus saves, because the Bible declares Jesus Christ to be the Son of God and the savior of the world. The Bible is the most hated book in all of history; it's also the most published.

The followers of Jesus Christ have been, and still are, the most persecuted people on the planet. Jesus is the most misunderstood, written about, and persecuted person in all of human history. Jesus Christ is the only man who is said to be the Son of God, raised from the dead, who is coming back to judge humankind and to rule and reign in His coming kingdom.

What you do with Jesus Christ is entirely up to you, but you should know what the most unique book in the world has to say about Him. Jesus Christ, by virtue of His life, death, resurrection, unique nature, and character, is vastly different from every other man who has ever lived.

Jesus Is Different from All Other Men

There's no other person who has been said to give you eternal life by believing in him. You can believe that George Washington was the first president of the United States, a famous historical figure, and a good man, but such faith won't save you. In fact, there's not one other person under heaven by whom you must be saved; such a promise belongs to Jesus Christ alone (Acts 4:12).

In this book, "snapshots" of Christ have been taken from the New Testament, where His person and work are clearly revealed. The Old Testament accounts of God and His will were revealed as a shadow of things to come. But once Christ stepped onto the stage of history as recorded in the New Testament, the very substance of God's plan was disclosed (Colossians 2:16–17; Hebrews 10:1).

John wrote that Jesus performed many signs so that people might believe that He was the Christ (Savior), and through believing they might have life. The word he used for *sign* might be rendered "that by which a person or a thing is distinguished from others and is known."

It's not by believing in miraculous signs that a person is saved, but by believing that Jesus is the Christ. Jesus authenticated the fact that He was the one prophesied about from ages past, the one who was to save His people from their sins. Jesus Christ did perform many miraculous signs by which He gave evidence that He is God in human flesh. However, the greatest space in this book, as in the New Testament, examines the transcendent character traits of Christ. It doesn't focus so much on what He did but who He is.

Jesus is unique because no other person is said to have been born to a virgin. In His birth, Jesus became part of the human race through His mother, Mary, but He didn't become sinful, because His father wasn't of the line of Adam. Mary was overshadowed by the Holy Spirit, so Jesus was born of God.

To question the virgin birth is natural, but it's doubtful that we have our calendar date set according to a mythical character, a fraud who would lie about His resurrection yet gave the world the finest moral teachings ever known.

During His earliest years of childhood, Jesus was exceptional. He exercised self-control as no other person could. Jesus's miracles are unlike any other person's in history. His life reads like a fantasy, but there's as much evidence to support His historical life as there is about anyone who is well known. Look up *passion* in the dictionary, and among other things, you'll find a reference to the sufferings of Christ.

Jesus defines self-sacrifice and unconditional love in word and deed. Jesus can't be compared to any other leader regarding His supernatural ability to comfort His followers, then and now. It's not just the first thirty-three years of Jesus's life that testify of His greatness, but the subsequent two thousand, according to His continuing followers, also give evidence to His resurrection.

A proper understanding of Jesus Christ gives meaning to all of life. In Jesus Christ we can understand the deeper spiritual meaning of marriage. Jesus embodies the idea that it's difficult to get something for the man who has everything; His beneficence is without measure and completely unselfish.

Jesus didn't give Himself only for a lifetime but forever, and by His internal goodness, His people will know righteousness, peace, and safety from all evil for all eternity. Jesus is transcendent in all His ways. The following chapters of this book speak about the glory of Christ according to the Bible.

Jesus is different from all other men, and so are all of His disciples to a lesser degree. True followers of Christ have had their hearts changed toward Him, and they see themselves differently.

The Christian is in an ongoing process of change and can identify sin for what it is: an offense against God. The Christian is able to not sin, but he isn't unable to sin; his state of perfection is reserved for death or Jesus's coming kingdom.

Much has been written about true disciples and their sacrifices, persecution, and transformation in life. Many true believers have made the ultimate sacrifice for their Savior by giving their lives rather than compromising their faith in Jesus.

However, there's a great distinction between a follower of Christ and Christ Himself. All the Christian can do is proclaim the message and pray for his or her family, friends, acquaintances, and the world. Christ has the power to change the world by changing the hearts of humankind, and He is changing the world one person at a time—but not all of the world.

There are false disciples of Christ, and they wreak havoc in the church and cast a stumbling block before the world so that Christianity is all the more despised. Christianity is made up of the followers of Christ, and true followers are distinctly different from those who only pretend to be Christian.

The people of the world are in a terrible state and don't even know it. It is one thing to question why there are plagues, wars, sickness, and death, but it is another thing to accept the harsh reality that these things point to impending and eternal torment. The true Christian is given an eternal perspective from God, by which he is enabled to see this life as passing away and pointing to an eternal state.

The Bible is a book of objective truth, which is meant to move a person from an understanding about Christ to a healthy relationship with Him. It is one thing to know *about* the person of Jesus Christ, but it is another to know Him. It is one thing to know that Jesus was trustworthy by the things written about Him, but it is another to trust Him for yourself. Trust is the element upon which all healthy relationships are built. Trust moves a relationship from superficial to meaningful, and it allows the recipient to know that he is loved. *Trust* is a synonym for *faith*. God-given faith unlocks all the resources of Christ, by which a man is saved, and only such a faith can move a man from knowing about Christ to knowing Him.

God-given faith involves a commitment to Jesus Christ. In our day we have lost the whole concept of commitment. Men and women say, "Till death do us part," and then they separate after a few years. Commitment is meaningless unless it is ongoing and lifelong. The whole point of commitment is that it continues; otherwise a man is just a hypocrite who says one thing and does another. *Foxe's Book of Martyrs* is an accurate, extensive, and historical account of men, women, and children who proved their faith in Christ by living out their commitment to Him to death.

One day all men will stand before the great white throne of God, the books will be opened, and the dead will be judged by their deeds written in the books. It is the dead who are said to go into eternal torment—or rather, those who are not found in the Lamb's Book of Life. There are those men who are given eternal life and those who remain in death.

> Then I saw a great white throne and Him who sat upon it, from whose presence earth and heaven fled away, and no place was found for them. And I saw the dead, the great and the small, standing before the throne, and books were opened; and another book was opened, which is the book of life; and the dead were judged from the things which were written in the books, according to their deeds. And the sea gave up the dead which were in it, and death and Hades gave up the dead which were in them; and they were judged, every one of them according to their deeds. Then death and Hades were thrown into the lake of fire. This is the second death, the lake of fire. And if anyone's name was not found written in the book of life, he was thrown into the lake of fire. (Revelation 20:11–15)

When God saves a man, He begins to change him. The God-given commitment of the saved is eternal because salvation is eternal. God-given faith is eternal because salvation is eternal. The person who knows Jesus is one who possesses both saving faith and commitment.

There are only two kinds of people in the world: those who know Jesus and those who don't. The person who knows Jesus has eternal life remaining in him, and it is that life in Christ that produces fruit that God approves (John 15:1–11). Eternal life is actually defined in scripture as knowing Jesus Christ. "And this is eternal life, that they might know you, the only true God, and Jesus Christ whom you have sent" (John 17:3).

To not know Jesus Christ is to be disobedient to Him, as found in Exodus 5:2: "But Pharaoh said, 'Who is the LORD that I should obey His voice to let Israel go? I do not know the LORD, and besides, I will not let Israel go." Pharaoh spoke from his heart what he knew to be true, and one day the lost will be judged by the very words that came from their mouths. The scripture tells us, "You brood of vipers, how can you, being evil, speak what is good? For the mouth speaks out of that which fills the heart" (Matthew 12:34). Unbelievers give testimony that they do not know the Jesus they need to know. There is the Jesus that people need to know, the one they think is Jesus but is not, and the one they think they know but in reality do not know at all. In order to know the Jesus of the Bible, a person must receive the Jesus that is the Christ.

This Jesus Is the Christ

There is the Jesus who is seen as a lucky charm. He comforts emotionally in times of affliction but is never thought about the rest of the time. There is the Jesus who is seen as a get-out-of-hell-free card, but there is no sorrow in the person's heart for having cost Christ the sufferings of hell. The true Jesus breaks the repentant person of his pride, convicts him of the sin that Jesus bore on his behalf, and cleanses him from the guilt that sin produces. The true Jesus creates repentance in the heart of the sinner, who then turns from sin throughout his life, as he ever increases in holiness and devotion to Jesus as Lord and Master.

You do not want to believe in the Jesus who allows you to go on sinning without feeling remorse, desiring to live a holy life, or loving Him. To be a Christian is to hate the sin that cost Jesus the fires of hell in your place. To be a Christian is to see your sin and to understand that it cost Jesus more suffering than you could ever imagine.

Two men go to see the movie *The Passion of the Christ*. One sits in tears as he beholds the sufferings of Christ, and he imagines himself as the one throwing all the blows and speaking all the false accusations. The other sits perplexed over the other man's tears. It is not necessary to cry over Christ's passion in order to be saved, but it is necessary to be moved to repentance in response to His sufferings.

The apostle Paul was a Pharisee (religious leader) who persecuted the church of Christ, but after he was knocked off his horse, literally, and brought to repentance and faith, he proclaimed the Jesus whom men crucified (1 Timothy 1:12–15). On one particular day, Saul of Tarsus (Acts 7) witnessed the martyrdom of Stephen. Like his Lord, Stephen faced down the false accusations of religious leaders and confronted their hypocrisy with the truth of scripture. His words were so gracious and yet so true about their sinful condition that his hearers erupted in an act of violence. At his death Stephen beheld the face of Jesus, and as if reflected in a mirror, Jesus was revealed to a young man named Saul.

At first Saul ignored the light of Christ as reflected in Stephen's death, but in time Jesus showed His presence like the light of the noonday sun. It was then that Saul (also the name of the first king of Israel), who was renamed Paul (meaning "small"), understood that this Jesus whom he had persecuted was the Christ, the long-awaited Messiah, the Savior of Israel and all people groups of the world.

In order to be saved, a person needs to receive the Christ of the Gospels, the New Testament, and Paul. The following are some key verses that reveal Jesus of Nazareth as the Christ, who was rejected by His own people, Israel, which represents the whole of mankind.

"Paul went to the Jews in the synagogue, as he customarily did, and on three Sabbath days he addressed them from the scriptures, explaining and giving evidence that the Christ had to suffer and *rise again from the dead*, and saying, *this Jesus* whom I am proclaiming to you is the Christ" (Acts 17:2–3, emphasis added).

"Therefore let all the house of Israel know for certain that God has made Him both Lord and Christ—*this Jesus whom you crucified*" (Acts 2:36, emphasis added).

"Let it be known to all of you and to all the people of Israel, that by the name of Jesus Christ the Nazarene, *whom you crucified*, whom God raised from the dead by this name this man stands here before you in good health" (Acts 4:10, emphasis added).

"For I determined to know nothing among you except Jesus Christ, and *Him crucified*" (1 Corinthians 2:2, emphasis added).

The common thread in the New Testament teaching about the Christ is that He was crucified. In the early church, Peter could say to those in Jerusalem "whom you crucified," because his hearers were those who had probably been there on that dreadful and glorious day. However, in reality, all those for whom Jesus died were there as surely as if they'd driven the nails themselves, because Jesus suffered on their behalf.

In our present culture, the word *sin* is despised, scoffed at, ridiculed, and ignored. However, it is a very serious word in light of eternity. Sin is the way God defines all the mischief that takes place in the world. Sin is the reason brother fights brother, neighbors gossip, the guilty lie, the lazy steal, tyrants kill, and all men justify their evil deeds. Sin is primarily the result of a person's broken relationship with God. Because men are sinners, they hate God, fail to acknowledge His existence, refuse to worship Him as God, reject His commands, and will not submit to His authority (Romans 1). Man will follow any false religion that allows him to think well of his own soul, and work his way into a good standing with God—even though his conscience is defiled and causes him feelings of guilt his whole life through.

When a sinner views his sin as not bad enough to merit hell, then in his mind there is no need for a Savior, and Jesus can become whatever the sinner wants Him to be. Man has always fashioned idols of wood, metal, and stone to his own liking and has invented religions according to his sinful desires. For this reason, when Jesus appeared He was rejected, sentenced to death, mocked, beaten, and crucified. Jesus's death was contrived by the religious leaders, whose hypocrisy was unveiled by Him. Jesus's crucifixion was carried out by the Romans, whose god was Caesar, because men love to worship men, and in so doing, they worship themselves.

The true Christian is one who believes himself to be responsible for Jesus's crucifixion. He understands that Jesus was crucified for him. The words "this Jesus whom you crucified" make perfect sense to him. He does not ignore the sufferings of Christ on the cross; they prove to him that God is a God of love and self-sacrifice who is intensely involved with His creation. He recognizes the transcendent nature of God, by which sinful men are judged and found extremely guilty. He understands that God is the source of all things, including all that is good. To ignore God is to ignore good, which explains the depravity of mankind. Jesus was crucified by all of us because He was good, but only the Christian accepts that fact as true and receives Jesus's sacrifice as his own.

To summarize this section, the Jesus of the Bible is the Jesus who identifies sin in all men. The Jesus you need to know is the one who died to remove sin and its penalty from your account. Acceptance and acknowledgment of sin is the issue that separates those who merely profess Jesus from those who sincerely possess him. If Jesus' crucifixion is not the central reason for His existence as a man in your own mind, if it does not cause you moments of great sorrow and joy, then you might want to consider Paul's admonition from 2 Corinthians 13:5: "Test yourselves to see if you are in the faith; examine yourselves! Or do you not recognize this about yourselves, that Jesus Christ is in you—unless indeed you fail the test?"

What It Means to Know Jesus

When I was in school, my neighbor Smitty introduced me to Fred when he came to visit. They had been in school together and were the best of friends. Smitty did not waste time in describing Fred as a first-class practical joker. He was the kind of person who could be expected to place a pail of water over a door to douse the one entering. No prank was too elaborate or too small for Fred to pull.

Fred had had a good friend named George when he'd attended school about fifteen years earlier. George was a very large, good natured, and kind man. One day Fred saw his friend George walking down the street, and of course he decided to play a little prank. So he snuck up on him from behind and gave him a huge slap on the back, which he was accustomed to doing. Normally after sneaking up on George, he would laugh himself silly to see a big man like George get so frazzled.

But when the man turned around this time, it wasn't George. This very large man looked down at Fred with a gruesome scowl on his face and said, "I don't know you." Fred looked up at the man and replied, "I don't know you either." After a pregnant pause, Fred explained the mix-up and expressed his sorrow for the slap on his back. The very large man understood the mistaken identity and could see Fred's sincerity, accepted his apology, and went on his way. Fred went directly home, entered his house, closed the door behind him, leaned back on it, and said, "I will never do that again."

The day is coming when multitudes of people, while standing on the very brink of eternity, will stand before the eternal Son of God and hear Him say to them, "I never knew you." And at the last, they will have to reluctantly confess, "I don't know you either." However, in their desperation to justify themselves, they will squeak out, "But we prophesied in your name, and in your name cast out demons, and in your name we did many wonderful works" (Matthew 7:22). Some, at long last, will come to realize the undeniable truth that they had not done those things in Jesus's name at all, that they had only deceived themselves.

The truth will be revealed in that hour that from birth all people are aliens and enemies to God, lacking any love for the Father's plan of salvation through His Son who fulfilled it. It is incredibly ironic that apart from God's grace and mercy, all people will go into eternal punishment without really knowing the one they rejected, despised, and alienated. He is the one person infinitely more loving than all others; He is truly worthy of praise, honor, and glory; and He could have given them everything they truly needed. However, fixed on running their own lives and satisfying themselves, they overlooked the one person they needed most.

At the writing of this book, my wife and I are in our fortieth year of marriage. The most intimate relationship is that of holy wedlock, where two people are bound together through a holy contract in which they pledge faithfulness to each other—for richer or poorer, in sickness or health, for better or worse, with only death able to part them. Together we have shared children, finances, home, bed, and problems of every kind. We have observed each other in every situation and have shared our hopes and fears, strengths and weaknesses. And through all of that, we have become intimate.

Intimacy can be understood as "into me you see." My wife and I have received intimacy through marriage by gaining knowledge of one another and reaping the benefits of a life shared together, which is infinitesimally small compared to a life shared with Christ. A life shared with Christ is a life shared with the one who can unlock the wealth and resources of God (Ephesians 1:3–23). In Christ there is knowledge of God that cannot be obtained any other way.

To know Jesus is to walk with Him day by day in a living relationship. There is nothing hypothetical about a true relationship with Jesus Christ; He is the most real person in the universe. As men we are all created; Christ is eternal. We are sustained from moment to moment by His divine hand; He is eternal life. The true Christian talks to Jesus in the good times and bad, and Jesus talks back through His Word. The Christian gives thanks to Jesus for all things, and he views all good things as undeserved blessings to sinful man. Sufferings work together for good to the Christian, because he understands that he is loved.

Christ is certainly better than some fictional hero, which is merely a figment of some author's imagination. Christ comforts in times of affliction, encourages in times of fear, edifies in times of doubt. He is closer than any friend is, more loving than any sister or brother, and wiser than any philosopher, and He always knows the right thing to do. Jesus proves the reality that the incredible book of the Bible is His Word. Many saints have uttered Jesus's words on their death beds, quoted scripture during the horrors of persecution, and been directed by God's Word when they did not know which way to go.

Knowing Jesus is an ongoing relationship. Quiet time with Jesus is not ritualistic; it does not follow the dictates of a systematized form of religion. Rather, it is a vibrant relationship with the living God. A relationship with Jesus grows the faith of the true believer. He enters into relationship with Jesus through the door of faith, and he continually deepens it as he walks from faith to faith. We observe Jesus's life in the Gospels, His love at the cross, His plan to rectify our hearts, minds, and wills at His resurrection from the dead. Our lives take a new course with Him as the center and the goal—and as the means to make it all happen as planned.

The Christ of whom I speak is a person of integrity. His quality of life is second to none. All men are unworthy to be compared to Him by virtue of His transcendent character. The Jesus of the Bible is the Jesus you need to know. If you do not know this Jesus, you might want to consider the Jesus who is described in the following pages, because He is the Jesus of the Bible.

The Godly of Every Age Seek to Know Jesus

The New Testament is the revelation of the Christ of God, the savior of men with whom God is pleased. The person who finds favor with God through Christ becomes increasingly dissatisfied with what this world has to offer, and he desires to know God instead. Such was the case with Moses, the servant of God. Moses was born Hebrew, but he was raised in the court of Pharaoh in the greatest nation in the world at that time. He was a learned man and a general in Egypt, according to the historian Josephus.

Moses experienced God's favor and blessing upon him and the nation of Israel. However, Moses was not content with just receiving the favor of God. By God's grace, Moses desired to *know* Him. "If you are pleased with me, teach me your ways so I may know you and continue to find favor with you. Remember that this nation is your people" (Exodus 33:13). Moses did not take for granted God or the favor he was privileged to receive from Him. After being saved by God, Moses turned away from living for himself and turned toward serving God. For Moses, the natural result of experiencing God's favor was a desire to know Him more.

Today when a man turns to God and desires to know Him better, he then becomes consumed with a desire for Jesus, whose words and works have been preserved in the New Testament, which teaches us the ways of God. To see Jesus is to see God in human form in a way that makes sense to a man. The life of Jesus is never to be studied for purely intellectual reasons but for the enrichment of the whole man. When the entire man learns of God in the way He is meant to be known, that man learns of God intellectually, emotionally, and volitionally.

Man has been made in God's image, and as such he is essentially moral in all his ways. In God's design, man is meant to be morally good, and ultimately in eternity, those who are brought into God's favor through Christ will be morally as good as God is. The morally good man makes a choice to do what is right in the sight of God. He must know what God means by good, and then he must be willing to do that good. The mind is the means by which a man obtains the knowledge of God's will; feelings can support or distort what the head comes to know. For this reason, a man's emotions must be included in the learning process. However, no matter how much a man learns about God, or how well his feelings are brought into submission, he is not morally good unless he is willing to do God's will.

It is the love of God in Christ that alone can transform a selfish, self-centered, proud, immoral man into a God-centered, God-fearing God-pleaser.

Within God Is the Heart of a Servant

"Jesus, knowing that the Father had given all things into His hands, and that He had come forth from God and was going back to God, got up from supper, and laid aside His garments; and taking a towel, He girded Himself. Then He poured water into the basin, and began to wash the disciples' feet and to wipe them with the towel with which He was girded." (John 13:3–5)

"Worthy are You, our Lord and our God, to receive glory and honor and power; for You created all things, and because of Your will they existed, and were created." (Revelation 4:11)

"There is the sea, great and broad, in which are swarms without number, animals both small and great. They all wait for You to give them their food in due season. When you ignore them, they panic. When you take away their life's breath, they die and return to dust." (Psalms 104:25, 27, 29)

**Jesus,
the True Servant Leader**

CHAPTER 2

JESUS, THE SERVANT GOD:
THE SERVITUDE OF GOD'S LOVE

There is a saying: "You are never more a servant than when you are willing to be treated like one." Jesus is unlike every other man who ever lived. He is God in human flesh, and He deserves all worship, honor, and respect as such (Revelation 4:11). However, during the time of His earthly pilgrimage He was not treated as God in human flesh. Quite the contrary, He was belittled, betrayed, denied, mistrusted, rejected, hated, laughed at, lied about, and dismissed. Jesus was willing to be treated like a servant—and worse—in order to reveal God to the world (Hebrews 1:3).

God is not a doormat, but He is humble and self-sacrificing—a servant. Jesus was not treated with the honor deserved by the Creator of the universe, but He revealed Himself to have a servant's heart by the way He lived among people who did not recognize Him as God. Israel had been given the scriptures that spoke of the coming of Messiah, and by this time His appearing had been anticipated for a very long time. One of His titles in the Old Testament was "son of man," which indicated how he would appear.

When Jesus was twelve years old, He stayed behind in Jerusalem so that He might converse with the leaders of Israel. His mother and father perceived Him to act contrary to what they were accustomed to, and they said to Him, "Why have you treated us this way?" No one speaks to God in such a way, even if He has taken up residence in the body of a child. Mary had been given evidence that her son Jesus had been born of God, because she'd given birth to Him as a virgin. When Jesus demanded full

16

commitment from those who followed Him (John 6), many walked away. But you do not stop following when you believe it's God you're serving.

It was at this time that Jesus fed thousands by creating a meal from nothing. When Jesus declared that it was in the plan that He go to Jerusalem to be betrayed, placed on trial, beaten, and crucified, Peter took Him aside, "manhandled" Him (literal in the Greek), and told Him, "This will never happen to you." This is not something you do to God.

Peter had watched Jesus raise the dead (Mark 5:35–43). During the greatest crisis of Jesus's life as a man, when He needed men for emotional support, they all denied Him, fled, and left Him to injustice. Out of jealousy and pride, all the religious leaders trumped up charges in order to have him put to death. The masses believed the report of their leaders and were willing to allow this great healer and teacher, who was love personified, to be killed. As a result of their accusations, the people came to believe that Jesus could not be the one prophesied to deliver them from their Roman captors, because He allowed Himself to be taken into custody. In His humiliation, Jesus was treated in ways no sane man would ever treat the all-powerful and living God. Apart from the eyes of faith, the world of Jesus's day treated Him like an unworthy slave. Some things never change!

The Son of God was ill treated the entire time He was carrying out the greatest sacrifice the universe would ever behold. His life was filled with this kind of irony. Jesus Christ lived life according to God's perfect standard, and He was sacrificed on the altar of God's judgment for human depravity. Yet wicked men—who represent the entire human race—treated Him as if He were a hell-bound sinner. Jesus Christ served humanity when He became a man, healed the masses in Israel, fed the hungry, and allowed Himself to be unjustly tried—though never convicted—and handed over to be scourged and crucified. Jesus became the greatest example of servanthood and injustice during the time of His human pilgrimage on earth that the world has ever known.

Jesus made it perfectly clear on the night He was betrayed that His people should serve one another as He'd served them when He washed their feet. Afterward He gave His disciples some very strong words of wisdom: "You call Me Teacher and Lord; and you are right, for so I am.

If I then, the Lord and the Teacher, washed your feet, you also ought to wash one another's feet" (John 13:13–14).

It is one thing to wash the feet of a fellow human being and quite another to wash the feet of God. It is one thing to be treated as a servant by your fellow human beings, but it must be quite different to be treated as such when you are the one who spoke all things into existence by the sound of your voice. Jesus was no ordinary servant; He was and is the supreme example of servanthood, because He alone serves creation as the Creator God. The greatest servant in human history was not merely a man but the eternal God.

Jesus, the Servant God

God opened the Bible, through Moses, with the words "in the beginning God." Furthermore, it is no coincidence that at the beginning of the New Testament, John's gospel also begins with similar words: "In the beginning was the Word." In Greek, *word* means "expression," and Christ is said to be the expression or manifestation of God Himself. Put another way, God's purpose is to make Himself known to those He creates, which He did perfectly in the person of His Son.

Jesus Christ is the revelation of God in human form; He can be observed for who He is by all who receive Him (2 Corinthians 4:6). In John 1:14 God declared, "And the Word became flesh and dwelt among us," by which phrase He made it perfectly clear that the Word who was in the beginning was the same Word who put on a human body. The apostle John then went on to show that it was by Jesus that God the Father created the world. "All things were created by him, and apart from him not one thing was created that has been created" (John 1:3 NET).

We know from Genesis 1:1 that God created the heavens and the earth, so in this statement from John it becomes perfectly clear that Jesus Christ is God who created everything. God thought it important for men to know that God comes first, a fact that man has been quite determined to reject, deny, and rebel against. After all, if God is first and all things came into being by His design and power, then He has all rights to the universe, including the right to judge what He created.

In the book of Exodus we are told that Moses stood before God, who revealed Himself in a bush that burned but was not consumed. When Moses asked His name, God declared Himself to be "I AM THAT I AM." It is in this one and only personal name that God reveals Himself as the self-existent and eternal being who was before all things. In writing to the church at Colossae, Paul declared Jesus Christ to be the self-existent "I AM THAT I AM" when he penned these words: "For by Him [Jesus] all things were created, both in the heavens and on earth, visible and invisible, whether thrones or dominions or rulers or authorities—all things have been created through Him and for Him. He is before all things, and in Him all things hold together" (Colossians 1:16–17).

There are two forms of life in the universe: created life, such as you and I, and uncreated life, which is God alone. An eternal, self-existent God, who is before all things and has created all things, is the only explanation that stands the test of reason as to how all things came to be. As stated by Aristotle, you cannot "be" and "not be" at the same time and in the same relationship. Therefore, self-creation is an argument against reason, as stated in the previous chapter. Only an eternal, self-existent God makes any sense in explaining how the universe came to be. In the context of our present thought, only the eternal, self-existent one who created all things has all power and all authority.

There is authority, and there is power. My car possesses horsepower and the ability to go fast, but the policeman possesses the authority to stop me and give me a ticket. The policeman's authority is designated by a higher authority, the United States government. God possesses ultimate authority, because He is before all things and possesses ultimate power. He creates from nothing, and He sustains by the same power. The universe cannot sustain its own existence apart from God, who is eternal life. The laws of nature are kept by the almighty hand of God, and apart from Him they would not continue.

God is the first and primary cause of the entire created order. He is the ultimate power of the universe. He is eternal, which means He exists apart from time, which was also created by Him. He is also self-existent, which means He sustains Himself, something the created universe cannot do for itself. All the laws that govern the universe, such as the first and second laws of thermodynamics, are maintained by God.

God is bigger and greater than we can ever imagine, and yet He serves us—individually. It is important to keep in mind that the Son of God is the same Jesus who walked the earth and washed the disciples' feet. The same God, who has need of nothing, is the one who was mistreated all the days of His earthly ministry when He revealed Himself as the Messiah of Israel and the Savior of the world. Jesus served mankind in creation, and He will continue to serve by sustaining it forever.

Now and Forever After, Jesus Serves

In Colossians 1:17 the idea is that in Christ all things *continue*: "He himself is before all things and all things are *held together* in him" (emphasis added). This could also be translated "continue." No matter what breakthrough occurs in the area of quantum science, the universe is held together and continues in Christ, for there is no power apart from Christ to sustain creation. To misunderstand the sustaining power and presence of God is to mistake the one true God for an idol made in the image of man and conceived in his own perverted mind. When man's life ends, all things continue to exist. God is not like this. He is not simply the creator of all life; He is the source by which all life continues to exist. Therefore, no life can exist apart from Him.

God-given reason led the ancient philosophers to understand this fact. "The God who made the world and everything in it, who is Lord of heaven and earth, does not live in temples made by human hands, nor is he served by human hands, as if he needed anything, because he himself gives life and breath and everything to everyone … For in him we live and move about and exist, as even some of your own poets have said" (Acts 17:24–25, 28).

God alone is eternal life, which means that all other life is not eternal in the sense that it is self-sustaining. Therefore, apart from Him no created or temporal life can continue. It is a hard concept to receive, because what we know from our experience is that we continue—that is, until we die. But death is something we deny until it is impossible to do so. There is a spirit of unbelief in all of us about our own mortality. By self-deception we choose to believe that we sustain our own lives. Only in a sober moment or in the face of a terminal illness are we brought to disagree with such reasoning.

Temporal life has a beginning, but eternal life has no beginning. In the same way, temporal life has an end, but eternal life is without end. Only eternal life sustains itself and is independent from anyone or anything. Eternal life is described in the Bible as a divine person who has neither beginning of days nor end of life; it abides forever. Nothing else in the created order lives to that magnitude. Everything else in the universe is breaking down. The universe cannot sustain itself because it is not eternal life; it is therefore sustained by another: the immutable, immortal, only wise God who sustains His creation continually.

God serves the universe continually by sustaining its existence, and as long as it exists, He will have to serve. God is true to His word, and He has said that His people will endure forever, which means He has locked Himself into sustaining them forever. "But the saints of the Highest One will receive the kingdom and possess the kingdom forever, for all ages to come" (Daniel 7:18). Somehow, I think, it is no small thing to sustain the universe, even for God. Jesus takes His service very seriously.

Jesus Needs Never Serve

We need to pause at this point and try to answer in part the question of *why*. By virtue of His perfect nature, God is complete and needs nothing, so why would He ever create anything in the first place? Since the creation cannot add anything to Him, why would He create anything? Because the creation does not exist for some need in God, even though it is for His glory and pleasure, we must conclude that within God there is the heart of a servant.

Before we ever get to the magnitude of God's love in salvation, we are first confronted with His divine service in creation. Because everything God has done and all He will ever do will add nothing to His divine person, creation itself is an expression of divine love and sacrificial benevolence. The greatest recipients in the creation are the created. In the creation, the heart of God is revealed: His undying devotion, selfless love, sacrificial passion, and—not least of all—His eternal servitude.

The reality that God serves His creation becomes heartwarming when we understand that the self-existent God needs nothing. God deserves all glory because He is self-existent, but the glory that we attribute to Him adds nothing to Him. Truth and reason demand—by virtue of the fact that God is complete and perfect—that we believe that nothing can be added to Him. Therefore, the whole of His creation, and man in particular, add nothing to Him. All the great things that have been done throughout the ages by the great saints of God have added nothing to the person God is. All the missionaries who have left home, heritage, family, language, and culture; all the martyrs who have sacrificed their very lives for Christ; and all the dear saints who dared to live holy lives—all have added nothing to God.

To be sure, God deserves all the glory for the good He produces in the lives of those who love and serve Him. Nonetheless, all of creation—and even the work that God has undertaken for His own glory and purpose—add nothing to His person. God has never, nor does He now, need anything. The entire creation is a love gift from the Father to the Son, for God's love was perfect and complete before He created. In eternity, the love of God the Father, the Son, and the Holy Spirit was perfect and complete.

The only recipients in the universe are the created ones, because no person or thing can add anything to the Creator. The Father has planned to give all glory to the Son, the Son has agreed to submit and obey the Father, and the Holy Spirit loves and glorifies both Father and Son. Notwithstanding, nothing has been added to God that He did not already have. God labored for six days to create everything, and after it was created He gained nothing in His person. God labored for us, and while He must receive the glory because nothing else is right and true, He is not one bit better for the glory and the pleasure He receives. God's benevolence is beyond measure and without comparison, yet He is not increased by it in the smallest degree. From the moment Christ spoke the earth into existence, He began to serve the creation, which is something He had not done previously. Prior to the act of creation, there was no creation. Hence there was nothing for God to serve.

The servant heart of God is not meant to create in us some perverted sense of our own importance but to humble us beneath the staggering weight of God's sacrificial grandeur. God's glory produces holiness; His love creates a desire for Him; His grace produces godly humility; and His endless servanthood recreates a servant's heart in His children. The heart of God to serve is never more clearly seen than it is in the person of the Lord Jesus Christ.

Jesus, the Servant God/Man

The quintessential person to live life as God intended is Jesus Christ. Jesus lived life perfectly in every respect. We read in the letter to the Hebrews that His sacrifice was offered to God without blemish, which means it was without fault of any kind. Therefore, it is able to cleanse the conscience of the beneficiary much more than goats and bulls, which were only ritualistic and a mere shadow of the cleansing that was to come through Jesus. Christ's blood can cleanse perfectly, because the life He lived was perfect.

"For if the blood of goats and bulls and the ashes of a heifer sprinkling those who have been defiled sanctify for the cleansing of the flesh, how much more will the blood of Christ, who through the eternal Spirit offered Himself without blemish to God, cleanse your conscience from dead works to serve the living God?" (Hebrews 9:13–14). In a sacrifice, an innocent one pays the price so the guilty can go free. Christ is the innocent one, and sinful men are guilty.

Jesus is perfect in every respect. Therefore, He is also the perfect servant. The servitude of Christ is mostly clearly seen in Mark's Gospel. Each of the four Gospels reveals Jesus through the writer's own particular focus. Mark's Gospel unveils Jesus as the tireless servant. One of the recurring words used by Mark is *immediately*: "And immediately after they came out of the synagogue, they came into the house of Simon and Andrew, with James and John" (Mark 1:29). Jesus was always reported by Mark to be serving or going somewhere to serve *immediately*. Jesus knew of a need, and He made it His business to meet that need without delay.

No one takes his or her job as seriously as Jesus does. Jesus lived a life like something you might see in a comedy; the surreal life of a person who lives to perfection for others would be comical because no one lives that way—except for Jesus. We should consider that the life Jesus lived and the deeds He performed were all done with the suffering of the cross ever before Him, yet He never so much as slowed His pace.

Jesus got up before daylight so He might have time to pray, but He was interrupted by His disciples, who said, "Everyone is looking for you" (Mark 1:35–37). So He departed and went to another place. He said, "Let us go somewhere else to the towns nearby, so that I may preach there also; for that is what I came for." Jesus did not become a man in order to live selfishly but to serve the Father's will and save sinners. To observe the excess—according to human standards—to which Jesus served others, we need only read from Mark 3:20–21: "And He came home, and the crowd gathered again, to such an extent that they could not even eat a meal. When His own people heard of this, they went out to take custody of Him; for they were saying, 'He has lost His senses.'"

There are biographies of men from the Great Awakening, which is a period of great revival in the history of the church, whose lives were tirelessly spent in pursuit of Jesus's will, church, and glory. Such men literally burned themselves out in early death because of loving devotion to Jesus their Lord. How different that is from today, when many blog sites teach how *not* to burn out for Jesus Christ. The motive and means for living tirelessly for Jesus is Jesus Himself. The record of His tireless life is found in particular in the Gospel of Mark.

Jesus's efforts were tireless, but that didn't mean He didn't take time to be with His heavenly Father. Rest for the soul is vitally important. No man can give without first receiving from God. It is one thing to rest and receive what is needed for the work—and quite another to rest in order to secure a long and selfish life. When Jesus rested, it was for the right reason, but He was also willing to spend Himself without thought for His own needs.

In the following case, Jesus taught His followers to rest for the glory of God and their own usefulness. "The apostles gathered together with Jesus; and they reported to Him all that they had done and taught. And He said to them, 'Come away by yourselves to a secluded place and rest a while.' [For there were many people coming and going, and they did not even have time to eat.] They went away in the boat to a secluded place by themselves" (Mark 6:30–32).

In the garden of Gethsemane, Jesus warned His disciples, "Keep watching and praying that you may not come into temptation; the spirit is willing, but the flesh is weak" (Mark 14:38). There is absolutely nothing selfish about doing what is necessary to avoid temptation and sin. Jesus secured eternity for His disciples by living perfectly so that He could one day live out His life perfectly through those who believed in Him.

Many are the qualifications of a really good leader, but an exceptional leader possesses the one quality that is absolutely essential to rule well: servanthood. Only a good servant can properly understand the people he serves. Therefore, Jesus is perfectly suited to rule His kingdom with love, righteousness, and fairness.

You need to know Jesus, because only Jesus can serve God as He is meant to be served. God created all men to serve Him with love and sincerity for His glory and pleasure. Apart from Jesus Christ there is no hope for sinful men to serve God acceptably, to fulfill the purpose for which they were created. All men serve one another to one degree or another, but all such service falls woefully short of what God requires. Only identification with Christ can satisfy God and, in this context, make man an acceptable servant of God.

WITHIN GOD IS A TRUSTWORTHY HEART

"And all who heard Him were amazed at His understanding and His answers." (Luke 2:47)

"And He said to them, 'Why is it that you were looking for Me? Did you not know that I had to be in My Father's house?'" (Luke 2:49)

"And He went down with them and came to Nazareth, and He continued in subjection to them. And His mother treasured all things in her heart." (Luke 2:51a)

The Great *I AM*:
The One through Whom We Live and Move and
Have Our Being, Submitted Himself to Sinners

CHAPTER 3

JESUS, A RULER WHO CAN BE TRUSTED: THE TRUSTWORTHINESS OF GOD'S LOVE

A trustworthy leader is one who has proven to be responsible by not asking more of his followers than he is willing to give of himself, who is humble enough to serve, and who is not tyrannical but loving. Concerning Jesus, Isaiah prophesied that He would be God Almighty and eternal. At the same time, He would be wonderful as a counselor (empathetic, understanding, kind), and He would be the source of peace rather than war in every possible dimension. "For a child will be born to us, a son will be given to us; And the government will rest on His shoulders; And His name will be called Wonderful Counselor, Mighty God, Eternal Father, Prince of Peace" (Isaiah 9:6).

Jesus's rule will be immeasurable, because it will be eternal as well as perfectly fair and just. "His dominion will be vast and he will bring immeasurable prosperity. He will rule on David's throne and over David's kingdom, establishing it and strengthening it by promoting justice and fairness, from this time forward and forevermore. The Lord's intense devotion to his people will accomplish this" (Isaiah 9:7).

Look closely at the last line of Isaiah 9:7, and you will notice the character and love with which Jesus Christ fulfills this prophetic passage: "The Lord's intense devotion to his people will accomplish this." Of the many things that could be said as to why Jesus can be trusted to establish justice and fairness, it is his intense devotion to His people that gives us the greatest reason. Look in the dictionary for the meaning of the word *passion*, and you will find this definition: "In the Bible, the sufferings of Jesus Christ from the Last Supper until His crucifixion."

In the lesson set before us, I would like to prove by scripture that Jesus Christ can be trusted to rule the earth for five very good reasons, five biblical truths regarding His personal character:

1. Jesus possessed the infinite power of God.
2. Jesus never abused His divine power.
3. Jesus entered puberty with a passion for God the Father.
4. Jesus's first miracle was not until His thirtieth year.
5. Jesus continued to submit to Joseph and Mary.

Combined, these five points make a composite picture of Jesus's childhood and reveal His superior fitness to rule as a trustworthy king.

1. Jesus Possessed the Infinite Power of God

It is one thing for God to exist in His natural state, and quite another to exist as a man. One of the foundational truths of the Christian religion is the fact that Jesus Christ is totally God and totally man. Jesus was as much a man as any person who has ever lived, but at the same time He was fully God. It is vitally important to understand the uniqueness of Jesus Christ in this way; otherwise, it is easy to miss His superior human character. Jesus Christ depicts the character of God, and at the same time He distinctly exemplifies what it means to be a perfect man.

There is no greater evidence that Jesus Christ was the eternal God incarnate than in His ability to create something from nothing. It is written, "Jesus then took the loaves, and having given thanks, He distributed to those who were seated; likewise also of the fish as much as they wanted" (John 6:11). Jesus took five loaves and two fish and fed five thousand men, or some fifteen thousand people, which means He created the food out of nothing. At that moment His disciples should have recognized Him as God. However, that truth was hidden from the people until the Holy Spirit began to open their eyes on the Day of Pentecost.

The fact that Jesus possessed the infinite power of God is incredible all by itself, but when coupled with the additional truths about Him as a child and young man, we must see Him as a transcendent person. Jesus not only possessed infinite power, but He never abused it as a child. The second reason Jesus can be trusted to rule is because He never abused His divine power.

2. Jesus Never Abused His Divine Power

"And the child grew and became strong, filled with wisdom, and the favor of God was upon him" (Luke 2:40).

In the 1960s an episode of *The Twilight Zone* aired on television in which a twelve-year-old child terrorized a small town. Imagine a child with the power to do whatever he wanted. Now imagine a vindictive and childish brat who insisted on having his own way, but instead of having a typical temper tantrum, he could do whatever he wanted to people. Scary, isn't it?

Jesus never acted like an average child. He never had fits of rage, fought with His siblings, or was even unkind to anyone. At the same time, Jesus possessed infinite power. The one who possesses infinite power does not experience consequences for his actions, because there is no power greater than his. Jesus could have done whatever He wanted in response to any evil He saw done to Himself or others—and there would have been plenty of abuse in Roman-occupied Israel in the time of Christ. However, there is no mention of any such action, either in the Bible or in the writings of any secular historian of that day. And you can believe that if there had been any uprising by Jesus, it would have been recorded.

Since Jesus possessed infinite power He could have done away with Roman rule altogether, made Israel a conquering nation, and placed Himself upon the throne. However, that was exactly the opposite of what actually took place. At a time when the multitudes were prepared to put Jesus on the throne because of His ability to heal and feed multitudes, His words were recorded. "And Jesus answered them, saying, 'The hour has come for the Son of Man to be glorified. Truly, truly, I say to you, unless a grain of wheat falls into the earth and dies, it remains alone; but if it dies, it bears much fruit. He who loves his life loses it, and he who hates his life in this world will keep it to life eternal" (John 12:23–25).

Jesus never abused His divine power, and neither did He sidestep the Father's will for His own comfort or prestige as a man. And even more incredible, He never abused His power as a boy. Think of it. What were you like at the age of six, and what were your siblings or your friends like? Did you or your friends ever lose your temper or get angry enough to fight or hurt one another? Do I even need to ask? Now, what would you or they have been like with infinite power? From what we know of the history of the world, what might a child do with limitless power? I think it's fair to say that the best among us, when given enough authority, can become mean when we are in a bad mood. We've all known young children who were bratty and obnoxious when spoiled sufficiently.

Now, think about a young child living in a land occupied by a foreign country, a land where soldiers were brutal and prejudiced, abusing their power at every opportunity. They took young women if they wanted them, and they stole from the needy through taxation, taking the bread out of people's mouths. What might a young child do—a good child who loved his family and his people—in such a case? Remember, there would be no consequences to a person who possessed limitless power. In the world in which we live, there is natural restraint when a person stops to count the cost, but what if there was no cost? What if, no matter how great the retaliation might be, a person had the ability to prevent it and/or send it back onto the heads of the enemy? Jesus of Nazareth possessed limitless power during all the years of His life, and He never abused it in the slightest way.

There is no one who is more fit to rule than the one who never abuses His power for selfish reasons. Jesus is fit to rule the universe, and He proved it as a human child. There is something exceedingly wonderful about the man who never takes matters into His own hands but waits upon the Lord and lives to do His will. Jesus is such a man! In His humility, He depended upon His Father's care and possessed the divine power to do whatever He wanted, yet He never abused it. Jesus is a person worth knowing.

The third reason Jesus can be trusted to rule is because He entered puberty with a passion for His heavenly Father.

3. Jesus Entered Puberty with a Passion for God the Father

It is impossible to comprehend to what degree Jesus submitted to the mother of His humanity, because no man understands what it means to be the infinite God. However, scripture records that God became a man, and as a man He submitted to His earthly parents for the thirty years prior to His ministry. Only when we compare Jesus's character and life to that of every other man do we see how far short man falls in his ability to live life with godly humility and submission.

Any honest person who has considered carefully the plight of man in history will have to admit that it has been very difficult for men to be submissive. A child needs to be lovingly disciplined in order to learn some degree of submissive behavior so that as a man he might become a productive part of society. Men are self-absorbed, proud, and hurtful by nature, which is why loving discipline is so important. Jesus never needed to be disciplined.

Children who are not raised in a two-parent home where a father and mother love each other will often have behavioral issues, and some may become violent. Human behavior can go to extremes, and there are many variables that contribute to the way men react to life's circumstances. However, the basic element in fallen man is the ability to react poorly to difficult circumstances. The question can then be asked: why doesn't man react in a more humble way?

Why don't men say to themselves, "I am not a good person. Therefore, I don't deserve any better than I'm getting"? Instead men often react to suffering by saying to themselves, "I don't deserve this." When people consider God in the midst of suffering, the most basic response is to ask, "How can a loving God cause me to suffer?" Sinful men rarely consider themselves to be the problem, nor do they understand that sin is such an offense to God that the suffering of this present world does not begin to carry out the justice that God demands. A lack of submission is the telltale sign of man's fallen condition. Jesus's willingness to submit to human authority, which is incomprehensible when we consider that He is God, is most clearly seen in the following passage.

Now His parents went to Jerusalem every year at the Feast of the Passover. And when He became twelve, they went up there according to the custom of the Feast; and as they were returning, after spending the full number of days, the boy Jesus stayed behind in Jerusalem. But His parents were unaware of it, but supposed Him to be in the caravan, and went a day's journey; and they began looking for Him among their relatives and acquaintances. When they did not find Him, they returned to Jerusalem looking for Him. Then, after three days they found Him in the temple, sitting in the midst of the teachers, both listening to them and asking them questions. When they saw Him, they were astonished; and His mother said to Him, "Son, why have You treated us this way? Behold, Your father and I have been anxiously looking for You." And He said to them, "Why is it that you were looking for Me? Did you not know that I had to be in My Father's house?" But they did not understand the statement which He had made to them. And He went down with them and came to Nazareth, and He continued in subjection to them; and His mother treasured all these things in her heart. (Luke 2:41–50)

It seemed to Joseph and Mary that Jesus was present in their caravan, but after a day they realized that they were mistaken and returned to Jerusalem to find Him. It would have taken a full day to return, which was why the story occurred over three days. Joseph and Mary were not negligent in their care of Jesus, and that is not the point of the story. It is important to consider the type of son He had been before considering Jesus's response to their inquiry. No parent ever had a child like Jesus, which can be observed in the words of Mary, his mother: "Son, why have You treated us this way?"

I have heard myself say to my son, and now I hear my son say the same to one of his boys, "Why do you always …," followed by whatever he did wrong. However, Mary's question was *why*. Her question was pregnant with the overwhelming truth that He had never done anything like that before. Jesus had never before caused Joseph and Mary to worry, complain, or grieve over His disobedience, insubordination, or disrespect, because He was completely devoid of such sinful characteristics. He was the quintessential perfect child, which is why this incident must have evoked much emotion in Mary and Joseph. Undoubtedly, they were filled with worry, because they had been convinced that He would never make such a choice; it was not in His nature to do so. They must have been convinced that something had happened to Him, which would also have been confusing because of God's protection of Jesus from Herod at His birth (Matthew 2:13–17).

Jesus's response to His worried parents is interesting, to say the least: "Why is it that you were looking for Me? Did you not know that I had to be in My Father's house?" Had they momentarily forgotten who Jesus's Father was: God in heaven? Had they forgotten to consider the one they were dealing with—the Messiah of Israel? Jesus reminded them who He was with a potent question and a phrase that is repeated throughout the New Testament: "Did you not know?"

The question is again pregnant with the immensity of Jesus's person. In effect, Jesus was saying to them, "Why are you looking for the creator of the universe? Don't you think I know where I am? Why are you worried about Me? Don't you think I can take care of Myself, seeing that I AM from eternity? Undoubtedly Mary and Joseph, like all of Jesus's future followers, would not completely grasp the significance of His full identity until after His resurrection. However, at this point Jesus set in motion a thought that would remain in Mary's heart for years to come and can be understood in these words: "And His mother treasured all these things in her heart."

Moreover, why did Jesus stay behind, remain in His Father's house, and converse with the teachers of Israel? The answer to these questions is bound up in two facts: (1) Jesus was twelve ("and when He became twelve, they went up there according to the custom of the Feast"), and (2) He went to His Father's house (" … My Father's house?"). At age twelve, Jesus had just entered the period of life that we know as adolescence. According to psychiatrist Theodore Lidz of Yale University, *adolescence* is defined as "the period between pubescence and physical maturity … the transition from childhood, initiated by prepubertal spurt of growth and impelled by the hormonal changes of puberty, to the attainment of adult prerogatives, responsibilities, and self-sufficiency." This quote is taken from INTRODUCTION TO PSYCHOLOGY AND COUNSELING, Paul D. Meier, M.D.

In short, this period of life initiates the transition from childhood and dependence to manhood and independence. The boy/man Jesus Christ was experiencing the biological changes that transition a boy into a man. At that time of life, all boys experience an independent spurt that drives their parents crazy because of sinful tendencies toward unruliness and disobedience. But Jesus was all about His heavenly Father's business.

The Father's will and its importance became very clear to Jesus when His biological clock turned mature, and He naturally responded to His parents' inquiry with the question "Did you not know?" It was as if He'd said, "Now that I'm a man, I need to be about my Father's business." Such thinking is not natural to sinful men, especially in a culture such as ours where young men rarely continue their fathers' businesses. Sometimes men do, especially when the father is successful, but most of us do what we want. Jesus, however, was all about fulfilling the Father's plan to save sinners.

In many places today, adulthood is recognized more by the right to drink, drive, and be independent than by the possession of good and godly character. Unlike sinful men who do not understand humble submission, Jesus was governed by the inherent presence of humility and compliance. It was not a chore for Jesus to submit to His heavenly Father; it was as natural as being God. Jesus Christ, the man, was defined by humility and submission, because His divine nature coexisted with his human part, and both natures were equally perfect and without sin.

At the point in the story where we read, "And He went down with them and came to Nazareth, and He continued in subjection to them," Jesus took humble submission to a whole new level. Jesus turned into a mature man with perfection and He did so far earlier than sinful men, who never really get there. Jesus continued to be compliant toward Joseph and Mary, and He contained His miracle-working power until His heavenly Father's appointed time.

The fourth reason Jesus can be trusted to rule is found in His patience to wait for God's appointed time.

4. Jesus's First Miracle Was Not Until His Thirtieth Year

"Jesus did this as the first of his miraculous signs, in Cana of Galilee. In this way he revealed his glory, and his disciples believed in him" (John 2:11).

The first miracle that Jesus performed was for His mother. "When the wine ran out, Jesus' mother said to him, 'They have no wine left'" (John 2:3). At that time He made this very clear statement to her: "Dear woman, why do you involve me? My time has not yet come?" (John 2:4). Jesus understood and declared to His mother that the divine purpose in doing miracles was not for any purpose that originated in man. Even the Son of God did not seek to satisfy Himself. Mary, the mother of Christ, undoubtedly sought the good of the bridegroom, the bride, and all the guests at the wedding when she desired that Jesus fix the problem of the wine shortage. But Jesus is not to be used by men, no matter how elevated the motive.

This is an important lesson for us to learn in this present evil age when the health-and-wealth gospel is so prevalent. Jesus performed the miracle of changing water into wine as a sign to His disciples, to reveal Himself as the Christ and the object of His disciples' faith—an eternal purpose. Jesus can be trusted to rule the nations with justice and fairness because, even as a human, His divine character and integrity were incorruptible, no matter how insignificant to the human eye they might have been. In life, He never misused His limitless power, even though to men it might have seemed good to grant His mother's request to care for someone in need.

Christian, let me hasten to add that it is this kind of life that is made available to you by faith. It is not a life of selfishness, greed, covetousness, and idolatry. No, it is a life of unselfish submission to the authority that God offers you in Christ. When life's temptations are beyond you, understand that God does not expect you to overcome worldliness by any human ability but by the life of Christ that is poured into your heart through the working of the Holy Spirit and by faith.

The character of Christ was proven throughout the course of His life, and it is that life and character that is made available to you. Because Jesus's life is made available through the working of the Holy Spirit, we are admonished in Philippians 2 to have within ourselves the same attitude that was within Christ. All the admonitions of the New Testament toward those who believe are based on the life of God that is made available through Christ. "You should have the same attitude toward one another that Christ Jesus had, who though he existed in the form of God did not regard equality with God as something to be grasped, but emptied himself by taking on the form of a slave, by looking like other men, and by sharing in human nature. He humbled himself, by becoming obedient to the point of death – even death on a cross!" (Philippians 2:5). What earthly king ever did that?

According to Gallup's latest poll, Congress has an approval rating of 20 percent, so we might say that the American people have a serious problem with trusting their leaders. Sometime in the future, a leader is coming who can be trusted completely, and for those of us who have already trusted in Him as Lord and Savior, it is nice to know Him. Christian, do you trust in the integrity of the Lord Jesus Christ for all your daily needs? Non-Christian friend, would you trust Him today for your place in eternity?

The supreme example of incomparable power and voluntary humility are clearly seen in the life of Christ. By virtue of His limitless power as almighty God and His self-ordained limitations as a man, Jesus infinitely surpassed every other example of godly humility. Jesus proved His trustworthiness to rule by His behavior as a child.

5. Jesus Continued to Submit to Joseph and Mary

It is one thing for God to submit to God, but it is quite another for God to submit to man. God completely reversed the proper order of submission when He turned His Son into a man. It is no small matter for God to submit Himself to the leadership of a man. The universe is under the care of God, its creator, and not men. Governments have been ordained to minister for God in caring for justice in the affairs of men, but one day they will be held to account by God for the authority they have been given. Men are to be subject to God and not the other way around.

It was one thing for the child Jesus to submit to His earthly parents; it was another for the fully matured Jesus to do so. We are told in Luke's gospel that, following the blessing pronounced upon Jesus by Anna when

He was presented in the temple as a child, they returned to Nazareth. We are then told this additional truth: "The Child continued to grow and become strong, increasing in wisdom; and the grace of God was upon Him" (Luke 2:40). Jesus passed through all the normal stages of development that every person does. He did not possess the wisdom of God as a three-year-old child; He had to grow in wisdom. Jesus was given the responsibility to understand man from the perspective of being a man in every sense of the word. Jesus humbled Himself to become a man, and in His humiliation there were no shortcuts.

Furthermore, we learn from this account that when Jesus reached His twelfth year, He stayed in Jerusalem and conversed with the teachers of Israel in the temple. "And all who heard Him were amazed at His understanding and His answers." At twelve years of age, Jesus's human mind undoubtedly superseded the wisdom of anyone else, but then the paragraph concludes with this remark: "And Jesus kept increasing in wisdom and stature, and in favor with God and men" (Luke 2:52). That Jesus was in the process of maturing, there is no doubt. However, it is probably safe to say that by the time Jesus was twelve years old, He had already gone beyond the understanding of all other men, and He was perfect and without sin. Submitting, therefore, to Joseph and Mary was a work of humble love and patience that only God could accomplish.

We are told that Jesus continued in submission to His parents, and the word used for "submission" is *hupotasso* in Greek, which means to yield to another's admonition or advice with a voluntary attitude of giving in. It implies cooperation in order to carry a burden. After Jesus matured from the state of a child, He continued in subjection to a man who was not His earthly father, and a woman who, although she'd given birth to Him, was in no way His equal. They shared a common humanity, and Jesus understood all their human frailties, such as being tired, hungry, thirsty, confined to a very small space in a body. He experienced the gambit of human emotions without sin, for He was almighty God.

There is no mention of Jesus performing any miracles, preaching any sermons, or making His person and work known in any way when he was either twelve or thirty. These were the years of humble silence. He worked alongside a man who was His father in name only, and He did so with perfect respect and submission. Because there is no further mention of Joseph beyond Jesus's twelfth year, it is believed that Joseph died before Jesus entered ministry. Jesus understands what it means for a family to lose a father. It is important to understand that during Jesus's time on earth He was experiencing what it meant to be human within all the circumstances that accompany life in a fallen world. During all that time, He was perfectly patient in not revealing who He was before the appointed time. He never took matters into His own divine hands, and He never fixed all the things He undoubtedly could have rectified as God. He simply went on submitting Himself to His earthly parents with all patience and humility.

When Jesus began His earthly ministry, He presented Himself in the synagogue and spoke to the people as a teacher in Israel. "And all were speaking well of Him, and wondering at the gracious words which were falling from His lips; and they were saying, 'Is this not Joseph's son?'" (Luke 4:22). The people were confused at His great wisdom, because He had never exhibited anything like it before. Furthermore, Jesus had never attended school or become learned through the regular process of teaching.

There is a gifting by the Holy Spirit, even today, by which men are chosen by God to teach and preach in the local church. Such gifting is not a calling by men but by God. It is easy to lose sight of this reality because education is such an integral part of modern society. Let us never forget that in the first century Jesus chose out twelve men who were to become pillars in the church. These men were not learned scholars, but they all had one essential element that made them qualified to lead in the church. "Now as they observed the confidence of Peter and John and understood that they were uneducated and untrained men, they were amazed, and began to recognize them as having been with Jesus" (Acts 4:13).

Once we embrace the concept of a calling and empowering by the Holy Spirit of God for ministry, it is equally important to understand that such men have to study in order to be approved by God. "Be diligent to present yourself approved to God as a workman who does not need to be ashamed, accurately handling the word of truth" (2 Timothy 2:15).

Confidence in God's Word is comparable to faith in God. We should never confuse faith in God, the life and ministry of Christ, and the Holy Spirit with faith in scholarship, which can easily become idolatry.

To know Jesus is to know the true source of humility. You need to know Jesus, because He alone exemplifies perfect godly humility. Jesus never taught people for selfish reasons. He never did anything out of a wrong desire for praise. Jesus was God, and all praise is due His name, but everything He did was for love's sake. As a child, Jesus proved beyond any shadow of doubt that He did not cling to His right to be God, but abandoned all His rights for love of the Father and a desire to please Him.

Jesus is the only path to godly humility. From childhood, Jesus never misused His infinite, divine power. At age twelve, the age of puberty, Jesus's desire was to be in His heavenly Father's house and about His business, carrying out His divine will for His glory and pleasure. Jesus, being God, continued to submit Himself to His earthly parents as part of an exercise in incomparable humility. For these reasons and more, we understand Jesus to be a trustworthy leader of incomparable proportions.

You need to know Jesus because He alone possesses the infinite power of God, and He alone never abused that power over course of His entire life. He patiently waited for the appointed time to die, and then He willingly went to the cross in order to fulfill His heavenly Father's will. Jesus submitted to His earthly parents, who were inferior by reason of being created and because they were sinners at heart. No man who has ever lived has waited to die the death that Jesus died, and He did so with perfect patience, submission, obedience, and love. Jesus is a man worth knowing.

Within God Is a Heart
of Submission

"I kept looking in the night visions, and behold, with the clouds of heaven One like a Son of Man was coming, and He came up to the Ancient of Days and was presented before Him." (Daniel 7:13)

"Behold, this child is appointed for the fall and rise of many in Israel, and for a sign to be opposed—and a sword will pierce even your own soul—to the end that thoughts from many hearts may be revealed." (Luke 2:35)

The Penetrating Love of Jesus

CHAPTER 4

JESUS, THE SON OF MAN: THE PENETRATING TRUTH OF GOD'S LOVE

The "Son of man" is a title used of the Messiah in the Old Testament. In Ezekiel it is used seventy-four times, where He is repeatedly sent to speak judgment to the children of Israel. "Then He said to me, 'Son of man, I am sending you to the sons of Israel, to a rebellious people who have rebelled against Me; they and their fathers have transgressed against Me to this very day. I am sending you to them who are stubborn and obstinate children, and you shall say to them, "Thus says the Lord God." As for them, whether they listen or not—for they are a rebellious house—they will know that a prophet has been among them'" (Ezekiel 2:3–5).

The Son of man was Jesus's favorite designation for Himself as recorded in the Gospels. Jesus's defining characteristic as the Son of man was that He spoke truth into people's lives. Jesus fulfilled the role of the Messiah as the Son of man perfectly.

There is no pain more hurtful than when we hear a person speak badly about us. Gossip with malicious intent is devastating, especially when the facts are accurate. There is nothing in the world that is harder to do than to be harsh out of necessity with someone we love, as in the case of an alcoholic. We all want others to love us for what we are and to think well of us. The last thing we want is for someone to think badly about us because of some fault or failure on our part. For these reasons, we all find it hard to speak truth to the people we love when that truth places them in a bad light.

Jesus, however, had no such problem, because He loved men perfectly. Therefore, He did not prioritize affection from others over their welfare. He always spoke with unselfish motives and thereby exemplified speaking the truth in love.

Such was the case when He performed His very first miracle. He and His mother attended a wedding feast. In Jewish tradition, it was a time when the groom would prove his ability to care for his new bride by making adequate preparations for the feast. On this occasion, however, the wine ran out. Mary, Jesus's mother, caring that the young groom not be dishonored, turned to Jesus, who was the best person she knew for fixing problems. She said, "They have no wine."

In the divine plan, Jesus was about to reveal Himself to His disciples by instantly turning water into wine. Desiring to reveal to Mary that their relationship was about to be altered permanently, He said to her, "Woman, what does that have to do with us? My hour has not yet come." The term *woman* was respectful for a man to call a woman, but it was not fitting for a son to call his mother. Mary was the mother of Jesus, but she was not the mother of God. Jesus would not so much as inadvertently speak or do anything that would allow a person to infer something to their hurt. Mary was an obedient vessel, and that was good but nothing more. Jesus was about to embark on a ministry that would reveal Himself to be the Lord God, the "I AM THAT I AM." It was vitally important, therefore, that Mary understand her proper place in the divine sequence of events. She had cared for Jesus as a child who had grown into manhood, but that was all behind them now, and He was about to take His place as the savior of the world. He spoke the truth, therefore, in love.

Mary could rejoice in the reality that her son was of divine origin. She had been exceedingly blessed with the task of carrying the Messiah in her body and giving birth to the one prophesied to come in ages past. There was no pain associated with her God-appointed task—that is, not until a later time when He would fully reveal the reason for His appearing.

The Penetrating Truth That Pierced Mary's Heart

The leading reason that a person does not come to a saving knowledge of Jesus Christ is an unwillingness to hear the truth about his or her human condition. Pride is the primary motivator in the heart of the sinner. It takes a serious amount of pride for sinful men—which we all are—to override the eternal, self-existent Creator. Furthermore, every action that overrides God's will is by definition sinful. If we want to lie, our pride tells us we can override God's will, which says that we should *not* lie; and we lie anyway.

Some people are weighed down with an enormous amount of guilt, but guilt alone cannot change the sinner's heart to submit to the will of God (Romans 8:6–8). It is possible for people to know their sin and realize their own imperfections in serving God—and still not bow the knee to God's plan of salvation through Jesus Christ. It takes a miraculous work of God in the sinner's heart to produce saving faith, by which a sinner takes God at His word, repents (turns away from his sin), and trusts in Jesus Christ alone for salvation.

Such a work was done in the heart of Mary, Jesus's human mother, which proves beyond any doubt that there is only one person in all of history who was born without sin. Mary was no doubt a believer before Jesus went to the cross. However, the realization of sin is an ongoing condition in the heart of the true believer. The cross brought the consciousness of sin to a much deeper level for Mary, and it will do the same for all those who will walk in her steps. At the presentation of Jesus in the temple, Mary met an elderly man named Simeon.

> Now there was a man in Jerusalem whose name was Simeon; and this man was righteous and devout, looking for the consolation of Israel; and the Holy Spirit was upon him, and it had been revealed to him by the Holy Spirit that he would not see death before he had seen the Lord's Christ. And he came in the Spirit into the temple; and when the parents brought in the child Jesus, to carry out for Him the custom of the law, then he took Him into his arms, and blessed God, and said. "Now Lord, You are releasing Your slave to depart in peace, according to

Your word; For my eyes have seen your salvation, which you have prepared in the presence of all peoples, a light of revelation to the Gentiles, and the glory of your people Israel. Behold, this child is appointed for the fall and rise of many in Israel, and for a sign to be opposed— *and a sword will pierce even your own soul*—to the end that thoughts from many hearts may be revealed." (Luke 2:25–35, emphasis added)

A day came in the life of Mary, the mother of Jesus, when a man looked her square in the eye and said to her, "Behold, this child is appointed for the fall and rise of many in Israel, and for a sign to be opposed—and a sword will pierce even your own soul." You have to wonder what she must have thought in that moment. The idea of a sword piercing Mary's body would have been terrifying, to be sure. However, it would have been even worse to think of a sword piercing her *soul*, which could go on hurting for a much longer time. Not many would live after receiving a sword wound to the heart, but if a person were to live, he would heal, and the pain would subside. However, a wound to the emotional heart would in many ways remain with a person for the rest of his life. The person who neglected to care for a sibling who was in an accident and was badly hurt or killed will carry the responsibility of that loss for the rest of his life. Many examples could be stated, and I am sure you get the idea that emotional pain, by reason of duration, can be far more painful than that which is physical. What did Simeon mean when he said that a sword would pierce her own soul?

It is not a difficult concept to understand that those who love others best are loved best by others. I have had the great fortune of being married to a woman who is truly kindhearted, who gives to the point that it hurts, who loves without holding anything back. For example, I have watched my wife on numerous occasions give our food away when we literally had very little food to spare. I have watched her behave this way toward countless people in the course of our marriage, which at present has been for forty years. I have seen people be not so nice in return, to be sure, but more often than not I've witnessed many people crowding around my wife with love and affection for her, and I know why. It's because she gives to others with no thought for herself. The natural response to an unselfish love is love!

Now, let us consider the earthly mother of Jesus, who is the Son of God, God in the flesh, love personified. We are told by John the apostle, "The one who does not love does not know God, for God is love" (1 John 4:8). The Jesus who said "I did not come to be served but to serve and to give my life as a ransom for many" proved His words to be true when He died upon a Roman cross as the sacrificial Lamb of God. Jesus was Mary's child, and He never acted like other sinful children. He was *never* disrespectful, *never* selfish, *never* unloving, and *never* unkind toward His siblings, other children, His parents, or any other adults. He was *always* submissive to His parents. In short, Mary had an experience with her son that no other mother on earth has ever had: she saw goodness in her son carried out to perfection all the days of her life.

Now, let's fast-forward thirty years to when Jesus entered into His ministry as an itinerate preacher. "And all were speaking well of Him, and wondering at the gracious words which were falling from His lips" (Luke 4:22). "The officers answered, 'Never has a man spoken the way this man speaks'" (John 7:46). "Some of the people therefore, when they heard these words, were saying, 'This certainly is the Prophet.' Others were saying, 'This is the Christ'" (John 7:40–41).

Judging by the response of the crowds in Israel, it is clear that no one had ever spoken as Jesus did. However, the fickle crowd eventually rejected Jesus because of His pronouncement of judgment upon them, and because the Jewish leaders made it look like He was weak before Rome. The Jewish leaders sought His death out of envy and fear of losing their positions in Israel.

Furthermore, Jesus had a healing ministry that was real and like nothing else the world has ever seen. "Jesus came down with them and stood on a level place; and there was a large crowd of His disciples, and a great throng of people from all Judea and Jerusalem and the coastal region of Tyre and Sidon … And all the people were trying to touch Him, for power was coming from Him and healing them all" (Luke 6:17, 19). "When Jesus had finished these words, He departed from Galilee and came into the region of Judea beyond the Jordan; and large crowds followed Him, and He healed them there" (Matthew 19:1–2).

Extensive healing was typical in the ministry of Jesus. Mary had to be acutely aware of Jesus's ministry of preaching and healing, as it was well known throughout Israel. However, it came to an abrupt end when He was taken to trial in the middle of the night, sentenced to death, and crucified. Then we read these words in John 19:25: "But standing by the cross of Jesus was His mother." Can we imagine how she might have felt? I don't think so. Those of us who have come to Christ believe by faith that He was perfectly holy and loving, but not a one of us has lived with Him in a family setting, which is the most intimate. Certainly none of us has given birth to Him. Mary would have loved Jesus more deeply than any other mother ever loved her son, and she had to watch Him face a kangaroo court, a deadly scourging, a malicious and humiliating mockery, and finally a brutal death.

Now, fast-forward another three days to where we learn that Mary came to understand that her son Jesus had risen from the dead. Her deepest sorrow must have turned to ecstatic joy. During the next forty days, Jesus appeared to His disciples numerous times. "Then beginning with Moses and with all the prophets, He explained to them the things concerning Himself in all the Scriptures" (Luke 24:27). Then on the Day of Pentecost the Holy Spirit was given to those who believed. "Now when the day of Pentecost had come, they were all together in one place … All of them were filled with the Holy Spirit." (Acts 1:1, 4a).

One of the great works of the Holy Spirit is to guide the believer into the truth. "But when He, the Spirit of truth, comes, He will guide you into all the truth" (John 16:13a). One of the truths that the Holy Spirit revealed was that Jesus bore the sins of His people. "He made Him who knew no sin to become sin for us, so that we might become the righteousness of God in Him" (2 Corinthians 5:21).

Now, place yourselves in Mary's shoes as much as you can for a brief moment. How would she have felt when she came to the full realization that her son was the Lamb of God who takes away the sins of those who believe? How would she have felt as her eyes were opened so she could fully understand the complete message about her well-loved son? Up to that point, these things had been hidden in her heart and shrouded in mystery. But as the fog began to clear and she started to see Jesus as she'd never seen Him before, she understood that God's wrath had fallen upon Him. The sinless, pure, holy, undefiled Lamb of God had taken the full weight of her sin's penalty. The full presence of sin's guilt, and the full horror of God's eternal anger, had descended upon Him—and it was for *her* sins that He had died. Oh, how the words of Simeon, hidden in her heart from so long ago, must have flashed across her mind: "And a sword will pierce even your own soul—to the end that thoughts from many hearts may be revealed."

Mary, the mother of Jesus, is an illustration of all believers who, upon placing their faith in Him, become keenly aware of how their wicked words and works have cost the Son of God more than they could ever comprehend. For Mary, there must have been moments from the past that flashed before her eyes when she had been selfish, wrongfully irritated, proud, and maybe even unkind to her son. And then would come the thought, *Jesus died for those sins too.* So it is with every believer. As a sin comes to our attention, the blood of Christ is there for the cleansing, washing away the guilt of sin, for the price of that sin was paid by the suffering of God's Son. It was the suffering of Christ that broke Mary's heart. His pain was the sword that pierced even her own soul.

Because Mary illustrates the broken heart that all believers experience when they become aware of what their sins cost the Son of God, Simeon concluded his thoughts with these words: "to the end that thoughts from many hearts may be revealed." The Old and New Testaments alike describe the hearts of true believers when they turn by the grace of God toward Christ. It is God whom we once ignored, denied, hated, disobeyed, and rebelled against. David recounted his understanding of sin so that we all could become painfully aware of our own wickedness: "For You do not delight in sacrifice, otherwise I would give it; You are not pleased with burnt offering. The sacrifices of God are a broken spirit; a broken and a contrite heart, O God, You will not despise" (Psalms 51:16–17)

After having Uriah killed (2 Samuel 11) so that he would not be found out for committing adultery with Uriah's wife, David took her to be his own wife. Eventually David was confronted by Nathan the prophet over his compounded sins, and upon hearing Nathan recount his ingratitude to God, David was broken and repentant. But it is especially important to notice the reason David was broken: "Let the bones which You have broken rejoice" (2 Samuel 11:8). It was not because he'd been caught with his hand in the cookie jar, so to speak, but because he had hurt the God he loved. "Against You, You only, I have sinned and done what is evil in Your sight, so that You are justified when You speak and blameless when You judge" (Psalms 51:4).

David, with an Old Testament understanding of God's suffering over sin, recognized the hurt he had inflicted upon Him. It was under that weight that David's bones had been broken, for he had hidden his sins from his own eyes and ignored their very existence. He was crushed in the depths of his soul. David had turned his back on the very God who had previously forgiven his sin and raised him up from shepherding sheep to ruling over God's people, Israel. David was broken by his own ingratitude and wicked behavior. He came to see most clearly how all his sin—which had been done in the sight of all Israel and had affected his children, wives, and servants—were insignificant compared to the hurt done to God.

I will never forget listening to a woman on the radio recount with tears and a deep sense of contrition that she felt her sin was greater than any other person's sin. The counselor on the other phone asked her what her sin was. She said she had killed her own child while it was in her womb. The counselor said she did not want to diminish the seriousness of what the caller had done, but that in fact the caller had committed a sin that was much worse. The caller could not believe that was possible. Then the counselor said to her, "By my sins I put to death the Son of God." The counselor had gotten it right, for there is no greater sin that that!

You need to know Jesus, because nowhere else on earth can you hear the truth more clearly. Jesus alone is the source of truth. He alone tells self-deceived sinners the way it really is. Jesus speaks the truth in love, He is merciful like no other, and He takes no pleasure in the destruction of the wicked. Jesus wept over Jerusalem on the eve of His death. You need to know Jesus so you can experience the truth from the only one who knows you better than you know yourself. To know Jesus is to be crushed under the weight of hurt that sin placed upon the Son of man. To know Jesus is to be set free into the light of His forgiveness and glory of His resurrection.

The penetrating truth about the Son of man is that Jesus Christ brings judgment upon the heads of all people through His life, death, and resurrection. He had to die, because sinners have to be punished. One of the hardest things to convey to a sinner is that he is worthy of hell. "I haven't murdered anyone," is the cry of the sinner who does not believe

THE JESUS YOU NEED TO KNOW

himself worthy of hell. Jesus did not die for the worst of sinners; He died for every person who would ever be saved. And every other person will be damned forever. The person who does not recognize his sin as great enough in the sight of God to send him to hell does not recognize his need for the sacrificial death of Christ on his behalf. Either Christ is received by sinners, or He is denied by the self-righteous; and self righteousness condemns people before a perfect and holy God. This is the penetrating truth that Jesus reveals as the Son of man.

The Penetrating Truth That Saved James and Jude

We all know what it is like to live among people while pretending to be something we are not, and how difficult that becomes when we live in the same house and share our lives in close proximity. For thirty years, five people that we know of lived with a perfect man. There was Jesus's stepfather Joseph, who is believed to have died sometime before Jesus's public ministry, because he was never spoken of in the Gospels after Jesus's twelfth birthday. And Jesus had at least four brothers, according to Matthew 13:55: "Is not this the carpenter's son? Is not His mother called Mary, and His brothers, James and Joseph and Simon and Judas?" These five lived with perfection personified. Scripture declares, "For it was fitting for us to have such a high priest, holy, innocent, undefiled, separated from sinners and exalted above the heavens" (Hebrews 7:26).

If the truth be told, no one reading this can even imagine what it would be like to live with a perfect person. We are not talking about someone who thinks he is perfect, for we all know what that is like, but someone who is in fact a perfect person. Jesus never lost His temper wrongfully, was never unkind, thoughtless, impatient, envious, puffed-up, boastful, rude, or unjust. Jesus never spoke so much as an angry word with a selfish motive. Furthermore, Jesus acted in this perfect way every day of His life, and before every person who lived in the same house with Him.

Joseph and Mary were witnesses of the miraculous events at Jesus's birth. They were visited by angels, shepherds, and the Magi, and they heard of the horrible slaying of children in their hometown and surrounding region. They were rescued by an angel through a dream in the night. Mary understood that she was with child as a virgin, and Joseph had it confirmed by an angel. However, these were but tall tales to Jesus's brothers. At the time of the feast, just before Jesus's ascent to Jerusalem and His death, we read of His brothers in John 7:5: "For not even his own brothers believed in him." To be sure, many people followed Jesus, but biblically there is a great, big difference between shallow faith and saving faith.

However, the shallow, non-saving faith of James and Jude would be changed to a saving, sanctifying faith and an unshakable calling. The apostle James was slain very early in the first century. "And he [king Herod] had James the brother of John put to death with a sword" (Acts 12:2). This probably occurred about AD 44, which means he would have already laid down his life for His Lord before the following events came to pass.

Galatians 2:12 speaks about an incident with the apostle Peter: "For prior to the coming of certain men from James, he used to eat with the Gentiles." These brothers had been sent by James, who is now considered to be the first pastor of the church at Jerusalem. "And recognizing the grace that had been given to me, James and Cephas [Peter] and John, who were reputed to be pillars" (Galatians 2:9). Furthermore, it was James who stood up at a council held in Jerusalem to address the brethren concerning Gentile believers.

So, how did James go from not believing in Jesus to being a pillar in the early church? We know he was present in the church as early as the upper room in Acts 1:14: "These all with one mind were continually devoting themselves to prayer, along with the women, and Mary the mother of Jesus, and with His brothers." It is further believed by many that it was this James, our Lord's half brother, whom Paul wrote about in 1 Corinthians 15:7: "Then He appeared to James." There does not seem to be any reason for either of the other two men named James to be singled out for an appearance by our Lord.

We are given even greater insight into this miraculous transformation in James from John 7. "After these things Jesus was walking in Galilee, for He was unwilling to walk in Judea because the Jews were seeking to kill Him. Now the feast of the Jews, the Feast of Booths, was near. Therefore His brothers said to Him, 'Leave here and go into Judea, so that Your disciples also may see Your works which You are doing. For no one does anything in secret when he himself seeks to be known publicly. If You do these things, show Yourself to the world.' For not even His brothers were believing in Him" (John 7:1–5).

If we connect a few dots, we get a very specific and ugly picture of Jesus's brothers prior to His resurrection. In verse 1 we are told that the Jews were seeking to kill Jesus. Then we are further told that Jesus's brothers told Him to go into Judea so that He might show Himself to His followers and not do His works in secret. Jesus did nothing in secret, but all Judea was going out to Him. He once had to preach from a boat so as not to get crushed by the multitudes. Everywhere He went, vast multitudes followed Him to see or receive a miracle and to hear His phenomenal preaching.

In fact, it was so clear to Jesus's twelve disciples that the Jews wanted to kill Him that when Jesus wanted to return to the grave of Lazarus they told Him, "Rabbi, the Jews were just now seeking to stone You, and are You going there again?" (John 11:8). Furthermore, we are told in later verses, "Therefore Thomas, who is called Didymus, said to his fellow disciples, 'Let us also go, so that we may die with Him'" (John 11:16, 18). There is quite a large difference between the concern that the twelve had for Jesus's welfare and the seeming lack of concern—or even worse, a desire to see Jesus's death—by His half brothers.

However, things changed. It is James's writing that opens the first letter of the general epistles after the letter to the Hebrews, and it is Jude's letter that closes the general epistles before the book of Revelation. In his letter James squared off with counterfeit Christianity, and Jude confronted false teachers. James defined authentic Christianity when he wrote, "Pure and undefiled religion in the sight of our God and Father is this: to visit orphans and widows in their distress, and to keep oneself unstained by the world" (James 1:27). In one verse he encapsulated the true Christian faith that is motivated by love for others. He identified true love as the good work of helping those in need, namely widows and orphans, as contrasted to mere speech that has no authentic work behind it.

And to complete the Christian faith, he marked out the world that lies in the lap of the wicked one, the devil, as spoken of in John's letter. He declared true Christianity to be a separation from an ungodly and disobedient world steeped in a wicked and contrary philosophy. True Christianity is action and theology at the point where they meet in truth.

Some have criticized James for preaching the necessity of human works, when in fact he taught authentic faith that is verified and made complete by the good works that faith produces.

Undoubtedly, James grew up in a righteous home where father and mother practiced faith in the God of Abraham and believed in the promise of a coming Messiah. But it had not changed James on the inside. Unlike his mother, Mary, who loved Jesus as well as any mother could love her son, he did not love his half brother Jesus, and he was no doubt envious of Jesus's recent popularity and fame. James probably resented His goodness and the fact that he himself was revealed as less than perfect and evil by comparison. Only this kind of contrary behavior could explain his desire to see Jesus return to Judea. The person who is not transformed by the unselfish love of Christ is destined to hate Him for it.

Nevertheless, the grace of God touched James so that the evil of his heart was revealed and the sins of rejecting the Son of God were forgiven. James was allowed to see, up close and personal, what counterfeit faith looks like, namely his own. Unlike his mother, who was probably a believer before she ever became the mother of the Messiah, James lived as an unbelieving Jew in the presence of the living God. When he was finally broken and allowed to see the wickedness of his own heart, it probably put Peter's cries after denying our Lord to silence by comparison. The end result of James's repentance and faith was humility and a love for Jesus, His half brother, who became to him his Lord and God. "James, a slave of God and of the Lord Jesus Christ, to the twelve tribes who are dispersed abroad: Greetings" (James 1:1).

James makes no mention of the fact that he was the half brother of Jesus Christ. There was no name-dropping on the part of this pastor, only a quiet humility born out of an awareness of his own rebellion and pride. It is always those who are forgiven much who love the most. In Christian circles we often make the mistake of looking for near-perfect people, but there are no perfect people, only repentant sinners to one degree or another.

Like James, Jude opened his letter with the same kind of humility: "Jude, a slave of Jesus Christ, and brother of James, to those who are the called, beloved in God the Father, and kept for Jesus Christ" (Jude v. 1). I think he goes one step further in humility and refers to himself as the brother of James—that is, the youngest of four brothers. Jude probably followed the same pattern James did, and when He came to His older half brother Jesus, He came to Him as a slave to the one true Lord. He saw himself as having no rights or privileges of his own, but he willingly followed his call to a life of self-denial, sacrifice, and suffering. He understood that he was beloved by God the Father because of Jesus Christ, and for this reason Jude would be kept for God.

When Jude wrote his letter, he first felt led to speak about the common salvation that all true Christians possess. However, the truth is narrow and the world is filled with false teachers who turn the truth of the gospel into a lie that uses the sacrifices of Christ as a means to fulfill their own sinful lusts.

James switched in mid stream, so to speak, and wrote instead, "I felt the necessity to write to you appealing that you contend earnestly for the faith which was once for all handed down to the saints" (James 1:3).

Jude did not take his faith as exclusive but saw a long line of saints who had embraced the truth of suffering for God in the midst of a fallen world. His was a faith handed down to all the saints, and it was handed down once. The truth is not your truth or my truth or even James's truth, but it is God's truth. He hands down the gospel truth, and it is the same truth to all, but only those humbled at the foot of Christ's sufferings can receive that reality.

You need to know the Jesus who lived among men as equal in humanity but superior as the God who created humanity from nothing. You need to know the Jesus who could endure the rejection of humans for thirty-three years or so—and then forgive it all by suffering in their place. He replaced their rejection with acceptance by being rejected of God Himself. You need to know the Jesus who could go up to Jerusalem because it was in the Father's plan to do so, knowing that His brothers wanted Him to go for all the wrong reasons.

Jesus went to Calvary's cross so He could turn the hard, uncaring hearts of James and Jude into men of courage who would call counterfeit faith for what it is—wicked. Furthermore, James and Jude were transformed into sensitive men who wanted their faith to work and help widows and orphans and not just be idle chatter.

You need to know the Jesus who makes a meaningful difference in people's lives.

WITHIN GOD IS A HEART OF COMFORT

"Now before the Feast of the Passover, Jesus knowing that His hour had come that He would depart out of this world to the Father, having loved His own who were in the world, He loved them to the end." (John 13:1)

"Then He poured water into the basin, and began to wash the disciples' feet and to wipe them with the towel with which He was girded." (John 13:5)

"These things I have spoken to you so that you may be kept from stumbling." (John 16:1)

Jesus Loved His Own to the Utmost

CHAPTER 5

JESUS, THE SELFLESS COMFORTER: THE COMFORT OF GOD'S LOVE

The unselfishness with which Jesus loved His disciples during the last hours of His earthly life is the main focus of this chapter. In our present world there are hints, reflections, shadows, and images of God's love, but they all pale into insignificance when compared to the love of Christ. Jesus's concern that His disciples would stumble and fall at His death seemed to outweigh His own coming trial, which is totally outrageous when we consider the trial He was about to face. Jesus taught the seriousness of placing a stumbling block before a brother (Matthew 18:6), and so He wanted to make sure His disciples would rise after they fell.

A stumbling block is something that is placed in a person's way that can cause him to stumble or fall. Throughout the ministry of Jesus, His disciples argued about who would be greatest in the kingdom of God. There may not have been malice in their arguments, and it was probably done unintentionally, but their rivalry had been placing a stumbling block in each other's way. They accepted the idea that the Messiah was going to rescue Israel from Roman rule, but they had missed the actual reason for Jesus's first coming. The disciples continued to be misled by teaching they had learned previously, even after they came to saving faith in Jesus, which is not uncommon. It is a lifelong endeavor for Christians to correct all the false teachings they've accepted as citizens of this present world. The disciples, however, threw a stumbling block in each other's way through their rivalry.

On the night before His death, Jesus spent a substantial amount of time telling all of them exactly what they needed to hear to keep from stumbling. Before He took them into the garden to pray, He first gave them the truth so they might place their faith where it would do the greatest good. Jesus warned them of their own coming failure but said that He would pray for them. Jesus told Peter, "Before the rooster crows twice, you will deny Me three times." Though Peter protested such a prediction, he still denied his Lord. When Jesus says that something is going to happen, it happens.

When the rooster crowed for the second time, Jesus turned and looked at Peter. At that very moment, Peter had, for the third time, denied knowing Jesus. I do not know what look Jesus had on His face, but there is no doubt that at some point Peter remembered Jesus's words: "Satan desires to sift you as wheat, but I have prayed for you that your faith does not fail." Peter was sufficiently instilled with the knowledge that he was loved by Jesus, and it was the love of Jesus that most effectively broke Peter of his pride. In Luke's Gospel we read that upon seeing Jesus in that moment, Peter went out and wept bitterly. In the Greek it literally means, "He wept *violently*."

When I was young and playing on the streets of Brooklyn, New York, during the 1960s, it was a common occurrence to hear a car roar down the street. One day I heard the loud roar of an engine, tires squealing, and the sound of a car racing just one block over, which was followed by a long screech and a loud thud. I ran between the houses and jumped the fence, and as I came out the driveway I saw a young man, maybe seventeen, leaning on a car with his head down, the body of an elderly woman lying on the ground. Another woman, maybe in her fifties, came out a door from across the street and screamed, "You killed my mother!" Even now it brings tears to my eyes. She ran toward the young man. He was in such a state that I don't think he could have defended himself, but two men arriving on the scene grabbed her and stopped her as she lunged toward him. Her scream was the violent cry of a woman who had lost the dearest person in her life—forever. It was the hopeless cry of eternal loss.

During the hours of Christ's deepest need, Peter denied Him and then lost Him to death. Peter's sin of denial had the impact of a sledge hammer upon his heart. There was no one dearer to Peter than our Lord was, because there was no one more dear. Peter was given the gift of looking into his own soul and seeing the selfishness that resided there in stark contrast to our Lord's greatest sacrifice. After going out from the presence of that horrid scene, Peter's words must have rung out in his head: "I do not know the man." Possibly he had spoken them within earshot of His Lord, who had turned to look at him. Peter's mind could not possibly process how he could deny the greatest man who had ever lived, but in the depths of his soul, he knew it to be true. Jesus's words must have crossed Peter's mind: "The hand of the one who betrays me is on the table," followed by his own words: "Lord, is it I?" Maybe he was able to distinguish between Judas's betrayal and his own denial, but either way, his emotions must have run deep and crushed him.

It is during the times of our greatest trials that Jesus's words hold the greatest comfort for us. During the second of two times when my whole world collapsed and I lost my job, house, and health within a couple of weeks, I felt I had nowhere else to turn but to Christ. On one particular evening I spent the whole night in prayer. I began at 10:00 p.m. and did not finish until 7:00 a.m. I concentrated on the book of James and John 13–17). It is hard to express the comfort given to me during the early hours of the morning. Faith was given as a gift, and I never felt so close to Christ. Jesus always speaks from the words of scripture, but make no mistake: He also orchestrates the circumstances of our lives that draw us close to Him.

On one morning during that same time frame, I had a rich sense of assurance come over me that everything was going to be all right. During my quiet time, I was reading Psalms 20: "May the LORD answer you in the day of trouble! May the name of the God of Jacob set you securely on high!" I know that in the proper interpretation of that passage the people of Israel are speaking, and they desire that the LORD will answer the king's request (the king of Israel); and the ultimate king is Jesus Christ. However, I felt such a nearness to God on that day that it was as if God, who had inspired the Word, was saying to me, "May the LORD (may I) answer you in the day of trouble. I had an overwhelming sense of God's love in the midst of very difficult circumstances. There is nothing quite like having a nurse startle you when she bends over your bed in the middle of the night and says, "I was just making sure you were still breathing."

On one particular day, I had a profound awareness of my sinfulness and unworthiness before God, but also of the love of God on my behalf through Christ. The phone rang, and it was my father. I had never told my dad about my stay in the hospital or any of my difficulties. I was a married man with a family, and up until that day, my father had never called me in the morning. He was a very kind man, a child of the Depression, and a hero of the second world war. He had been softened in a good way through the difficulties of life. My father was very introverted; he did not give hugs, and he never said "I love you." However, I have never felt more loved by a man as I did by my father. His sincerity was off the charts.

On that particular day, my father said to me, "I just wanted to say I love you." I said, "I know dad," after he hung up, and then I began to cry. It was as if God was saying to me, I just want you to be absolutely sure how much I love you. God speaks to us in so many ways, always most directly and with perfect accuracy from His holy Word, but also through the circumstances of life. He tells us that, as sinful men, we don't deserve the blessings we receive, but He loves us if we are joined to His Son, Jesus, through faith. When trials come and we must go through them, they are for our good and His glory, and the God of all the earth will always do what's right.

Jesus's Words of Comfort

"Now before the Feast of the Passover, Jesus knowing that His hour had come that He would depart out of this world to the Father, having loved His own who were in the world, He loved them to the end" (John 13:1)

We are told in this verse that Jesus loved His disciples to the end, or in some translations "to the utmost." The actual word in the Greek is *telos*, which might be interpreted as the limit of a thing, when it ceases to be. It could also be stated as everything a person is. So the apostle John was telling us that Jesus loved His disciples all the way to His earthly death with everything He was. In light of John's opening statement, which declares the overwhelming beneficence of Jesus Christ, we are further told that on the night that Jesus was betrayed He spent His last hours comforting, supporting, encouraging, and enlightening His disciples about the hour that was coming upon them. He did these things for His disciples so that they might be kept from stumbling. "These things I have spoken to you so that you may be kept from stumbling" (John 16:1).

Jesus had not settled into any form of self-pity, though He above all other men could have been tempted to. Instead He looked to lift up others. He could have become emotionally crippled by the horrors of crucifixion, but instead He could say, "Let not your heart be troubled, neither let it be afraid," just as His own faith was standing sure. He could have beckoned His disciples to console Him in the hours leading up to His suffering, a suffering that no other man could even imagine, let alone endure. Instead He spent most of His time counseling them about their upcoming loss and failure. The only thing Jesus asked of His disciples during the hours preceding His sacrificial death was their prayers. He agonized in the garden, suffered for resolve to do the Father's will, agonized for His own faithfulness, and sweat great drops of blood to put aside His own will. Jesus did all this while His disciples slept because they were weakened by self-confidence and pride, sorrow for their own temporary loss, and even a lack of faith in the Lord.

Jesus had a specific purpose for the upper-room discourse with its grand teachings, rich promises, and crucial admonitions. His disciples were facing a severe trial regarding their faith, which we see in Jesus's statement to Simon. "'Simon, Simon, behold, Satan has demanded permission to sift you like wheat; but I have prayed for you, that your faith may not fail; and you, when once you have turned again, strengthen your brothers.' But he said to Him, 'Lord, with You I am ready to go both to prison and to death!' And He said, 'I say to you, Peter, the rooster will not crow today until you have denied three times that you know Me'" (Luke 22:31–34).

Jesus told Peter that He had prayed that Peter's faith would not fail, so Jesus made it clear to Peter at that time that his faith was to be tested and was at risk of failing him. So it is from time to time for those of us who are Christians. We likewise are tested with regard to the stability of our faith. Peter, of course, was quite certain that he was willing to die for Jesus, but Jesus had to set him straight concerning the actual condition of his faith. Apart from Jesus's prayers for him, Peter was very vulnerable. When Jesus told Peter that he should strengthen his brothers after he repented of his own failures, he was reassuring Peter of His unconditional love. Furthermore, Jesus directed Peter to strengthen his brethren because they too would be in danger of losing their faith when Jesus was taken from them. They would scatter out of fear, and later their hearts would be filled with sorrow and loss.

The disciples were expecting the kingdom of the long-awaited Messiah to come during their day. They expected to sit and rule with Christ. What a letdown when that didn't happen. We can imagine that they were crushed in spirit, wrecked emotionally, and disappointed beyond belief, but most of all they had lost the one person who had come to define for them the meaning of life, love, purpose, direction, and perhaps most of all—hope. Jesus was going to be taken from them, so He prepared them for the coming trial through His discourse during the Last Supper (John 13) and His high-priestly prayer (John 17).

In John 14:1 Jesus admonished His disciples to have a trouble-free heart through faith in Him: "Do not let your heart be troubled; believe in God, believe also in Me." Jesus told them to have faith in Him as their ancestors had had faith in God. God had been faithful to men of faith (Hebrews 11), and now Jesus promised the same faithfulness to those who believed Him to be equal with God. "In You our fathers trusted; they trusted and You delivered them. To You they cried out and were delivered; in You they trusted and were not disappointed. But I am a worm and not a man, a reproach of men and despised by the people" (Psalms 22:4–6).

How ironic it is that Jesus admonished His disciples to have faith in Him, knowing that He would be made to feel as though He were not even a man but only a worm. The psalmist revealed Christ's thoughts when, because of the cruelty of mankind as represented by the populace at the cross, He understood Himself to be despised and reproached. Men treated Him with contempt and despised Him for making Himself out to be the Savior.

Jesus had never sought the applause of men. In fact, He had repeatedly run from it. He knew the reason He had come, and He made sure that men did not crown Him king to fulfill their own earthly lusts. He sought the will of the Father, which meant that His righteous life, which should have been free from suffering and death, would be offered in place of those who would reproach Him. Truly, He comforted His followers with a completely unselfish motive.

In John 14:18 He promised to return to His eleven remaining disciples as a parent. "I will not leave you as orphans; I will come to you." Jesus said

He would not leave them as orphans when He Himself stood upon the very precipice of abandonment by the Father, because He would take their place by bearing the punishment of their sins. This same substitution of a beloved child for forsaken orphans is true for all who follow Jesus. With no thought for Himself or the evil that was about to come upon Him, He promised that as a parent He would be faithful to them. His promise came to them only hours before He would experience the Father's complete withdrawal from Him, which would cause Him to cry out, "My God, my God, why have You forsaken me?" (Psalms 22:1).

In John 14:27 Jesus told them that He was leaving His peace with them, and unlike the world, He would never take it back. "Peace I leave with you; My peace I give to you; not as the world gives do I give to you. Do not let your heart be troubled, nor let it be fearful." But never did a person have less peace than Jesus did at the time of His death. "But He was pierced through for our transgressions, he was crushed for our iniquities; the chastening for our well-being fell upon Him, and by His scourging we are healed" (Isaiah 53:5).

Jesus is the Prince of Peace. Throughout eternity past, He existed as the one true and only God, in perfect peace within Himself, all-powerful in His glory and untouched by sin or anything that defiles. Before time was created, during an incomprehensible eternity, He was without distress of any kind. And yet Jesus willingly departed from His eternal state and bore the wrath of God.

In John 15:3 Jesus told the eleven disciples that they were already clean because of the word He'd spoken to them: love. He spoke of His care for them and said that their security rested in Him and His love for them. Every admonition, promise, consolation, and teaching of Jesus was a word of love at a most meaningful time. Then again in John 15:11 Jesus gave His reason for telling them all these things: "These things I have spoken to you so that My joy may be in you, and that your joy may be made full." Jesus wanted them to have His joy, a joy that would not be dependent on circumstances; and in light of their upcoming crisis, they would become very aware that they did not yet possess such a joy.

Jesus desired that His disciples experience unending joy at a time when He would experience incomprehensible grief. "I am poured out like water, and all my bones are out of joint; My heart is like wax; It is melted within me. My strength is dried up like a potsherd, and my tongue cleaves to my jaws; and You lay me in the dust of death" (Psalms 22:14–15). The greatest substitutionary sacrifice was made when Jesus hung upon a Roman cross; He was defiled so that His disciples might have joy.

Furthermore, He compared the love He had for them with the love the Father had for Him. "Just as the Father has loved Me, I have also loved you; abide in My love" (John 15:9). Since He was the long-awaited Messiah and chosen one of Israel, the disciples considered Him most beloved of the Father. Following Jesus's arrest, they certainly would have questioned their love for Him. They needed to be assured of Jesus's love for them, not because He hadn't adequately proved His love for them throughout the previous three years, but because they were about to have their blinders removed and their selfishness, fear, and competitive pride revealed. Jesus's love for them was not based on any merit in them but solely upon the goodness of His grace. This too would be revealed through the lessons of the cross and the hours preceding it.

Then in John 16:5–7 Jesus told His disciples that He would send them the Holy Spirit who would be an indispensible help to them. The Holy Spirit could only be sent to them if Jesus went away, which meant that even though He was leaving physically, He would return to them through the ministry of the Holy Spirit. "But now I am going to Him who sent Me; and none of you asks Me, 'Where are You going?' But because I have said these things to you, sorrow has filled your heart. But I tell you the truth, it is to your advantage that I go away; for if I do not go away, the Helper will not come to you; but if I go, I will send Him to you."

Jesus was about to be hung upon a cross, suspended, as it were, between heaven and earth, and separated from God and men. Jesus did not want His disciples to be left alone, even though He was about to be left alone like no man had ever been. He was mocked by some men, denied by others, betrayed by one, and afflicted by the Father who could inflict suffering like no other. Jesus loved His disciples more than any person has ever been loved. No person's sufferings can be compared to the sufferings of Christ. Therefore, Jesus's love for His disciples at the time of His death was infinitely greater than the love of any other man or woman.

In John 16:22–23 Jesus assured them of His continuing love, saying, "Therefore you too have grief now; but I will see you again, and your heart will rejoice, and no one will take your joy away from you." They were going to fail Him, but He would never fail them or retract His love from them. At the very time when Jesus sacrificed His joy for sinners' grief, His disciples fled and left Him alone. But they remembered His words when He returned to them and were absolutely assured of His steadfast and unconditional love for them. How meaningful the following words must have become to Jesus's disciples: "As a result of the anguish of His soul, He will see it and be satisfied; by His knowledge the Righteous One, My Servant, will justify the many, as He will bear their iniquities" (Isaiah 53:11). It is the love of Jesus Christ that gives the truest meaning to the word *grace*. In God's economy, grace is the undeserved justification of sins by the substitutionary sacrifice of His beloved Son.

In John 16:23 Jesus promised His disciples power in prayer through identification with Him. This was reflected in His words to His disciples on the eve of His death: "In that day you will not question Me about anything. Truly, truly, I say to you, if you ask the Father for anything in My name, He will give it to you." Jesus comforted His disciples through the promise that God the Father was going to answer their prayers in Jesus's name, a promise that had to have special significance when they looked back at their own denial of the Father's Son.

Everything Jesus said on the night of His death was meant to give His disciples hope. Whether it was His grand teachings, rich promises, or crucial admonitions, the goal was always the same: to secure their faith and guarantee that they understood that Jesus was not going to leave them permanently.

Jesus's Act of Comfort

John 16:1 is a very important verse to help us understand the events leading up to Jesus's arrest: "These things I have spoken to you so that you may be kept from stumbling." In this verse Jesus declared the reason for His discourse at that time: that they might be kept from stumbling. The word translated "kept from stumbling or falling away" in other translations is the Greek word **Skandalizó** *skan-dal-id'-zo*, which means "to put a stumbling block in the way upon which another may trip and fall." However, it can also mean causing a person to begin to distrust and desert one whom he ought to trust and obey. Furthermore, it can also mean seeing in someone what I disapprove of and what hinders me from acknowledging his authority. The most destructive force in any person's heart is a misunderstanding of who Christ is and what He came to accomplish, because it is at that point that falling away occurs.

Falling away has to do with one's proximity to Christ. The Christian who is close enough to see the Lord is close enough to be strengthened by Him. Jesus made this truth plain when He said to His disciples, "But these things I have spoken to you, so that when their hour comes, you may remember that I told you of them. These things I did not say to you at the beginning, because I was with you" (John 16:4). In the upper room He made it clear that He had not warned them about the upcoming persecution because He was with them.

What was true of His disciples continues to be true today, which is why it is so important for every Christian to develop "God-awareness," as the Puritans used to think of it. It is so easy to become isolated from Christ, even as a true Christian. I am speaking to those who are born-again and have received the saving work of Jesus, the Lord, into their hearts. Reading our Bibles out of duty and studying the scriptures without seeing the words of God coming to us at that very moment can make times of worship dry and keep us isolated from the person of Christ. The very reason for worship is for us to draw near to Christ for faith and strength.

When Jesus was about to leave His disciples, He protected them by intercessory prayer and teaching, and He gave them promises to strengthen their faith. We might understand that Jesus made Himself more near to His disciples on the eve of His death so they might endure the coming test of their faith. Jesus wanted His disciples to know that His death was not outside the plan, and for this reason He prophesied all the things that would come to pass. Furthermore, He wanted to instill in their hearts that He had voluntarily humbled himself in becoming a man, even to the point of death. "So when He had washed their feet, and taken His garments and reclined at the table again, He said to them, "Do you know what I have done to you? You call Me Teacher and Lord; and you are right, for so I am" (John 13:12–13).

He was saying that the great I AM, the Lord of all glory, had washed their feet, which was another way to convey to them that His death was part of His humility. It was willful and planned, and it did not take Him by surprise. They could take comfort in the fact that He was Lord, the sovereign of the universe, and He was in control.

It is always important for the Christian to hold the two sides of Jesus in perfect balance in his mind and heart; on the one side Jesus is meek and lowly, and on the other He is the one true and living God of the universe who does not bow to man. Jesus had the power to calm a raging storm with a word, and yet He was so gentle and intimate with His disciples that Peter could say to Him, "Never shall you wash my feet!" So endearing and desirable was Jesus that Peter—the impetuous, big, proud, rough-and-ready fisherman—heard Jesus say, "If I do not wash you, you have no part with Me." And he responded, "Lord, wash not only my feet, but also my hands and my head." On the one hand, Peter was appalled by the thought of Jesus—the one who healed multitudes, walked on water, and calmed a storm—washing his feet. At the same time, Jesus, who always had love in His eyes, kindness on His lips, and warmth in His heart, could cause Peter to do whatever He said, even if it meant washing his feet. There is no substitute for an intimate relationship with Jesus Christ, which is built upon the precise teaching of His Word, because it keeps to the two sides of Jesus in perfect balance.

When Jesus washed His disciples' feet, He revealed to them His humility so they might understand that He had stepped down voluntarily for their sakes. But most importantly, He did it to graphically demonstrate the extent to which He was willing to descend in order to love them. Jesus did this for the stability of their faith, because He was about to be taken into custody by men, beaten, tried, and murdered. He wanted to make it clear that these things did not happen to Him because He was weak. It was strength that sent Jesus to the cross, the strength of love that grows out of justice, truth, and self-sacrifice. Jesus knew that the first question that would go through His disciples' minds would be, "How does the great I AM and Creator of the universe get murdered by men? How does our Savior get beaten to a pulp?"

This was no small matter. His disciples were going to witness His death at the hands of sinful men, but Jesus had prepared them beforehand by letting them know that He knew what was going to take place. He had prayed for the perseverance of their faith and had assured them that He was in control of all things, that He had determined how all things were going to turn out. For this reason, He said to them, "These things I have spoken to you so that you may be kept from stumbling" (John 16:1). But Jesus was looking beyond the twelve apostles to the church age when He went on to say, "They will make you outcasts from the synagogue, but an hour is coming for everyone who kills you to think that he is offering service to God" (John 16:2). The words that were meant to comfort the twelve and strengthen their faith are equally important to His followers today, because apart from Him, we are weak at best.

"The best men among us are men at best" is a proverb that adequately describes the material with which Christ chose to build His church, and for this reason it is vitally important that men be filled with the Holy Spirit so they will be empowered, directed, and enlightened by God Himself, who alone can compensate for our shortcomings. Jesus understood this need, and on the night in which He was betrayed, He did what was necessary to ensure that His followers would not be broken beyond repair. Down through the centuries, godly men have made monumental mistakes, taught wrong doctrine, and lost their faith temporarily, but Jesus will never allow such falling away in His beloved to reach the point of losing salvation.

In preparing the disciples for His death, Jesus was also preparing them for the persecution they would face as His followers. We are told by the apostle Paul, "Indeed, all who desire to live godly in Christ Jesus will be persecuted" (2 Timothy 3:12). The New Testament is filled with the sufferings of the saints who entered into the sufferings of Christ for the gospel's sake. The idea of having a better life now, a heresy that some teach, is completely foreign to the New Testament account. The abundant life that the gospel presents is an internal one that includes a willingness to endure suffering. Unselfish suffering for the sake of others is what the Bible calls the abundant life. "The thief comes only to steal and kill and destroy; I came that they may have life, and have it abundantly" (John 10:10). False teachers steal away false converts to Christ, kill the deficient faith that is in them, and destroy any testimony of God's grace.

Christ foretold His own betrayal, which is found in John 13:21: "Truly, truly, I say to you, that one of you will betray Me." In this He exemplified and defined love as a willingness to be betrayed, rejected, and used by others with no thought of personal revenge. He taught His disciples to love as He defined it. He told them, "Love one another, even as I have loved you" (John 15:12). Apart from His saving grace, they were rebellious, wicked sinners who would have cried for His death along with the others. Regardless of their previous sinful condition, He forgave them, and for three years He taught them about His coming kingdom, the way they should live, their need for intimate dependence upon Him, and the faith necessary to keep them from stumbling.

The problem with following Jesus is that man can no more walk in Jesus's steps than a dog can walk as a man. For this reason, it was important for Jesus to reveal to Peter the actual state of his heart, the weakness of his resolve, and the instability of his faith apart from Jesus's intercessory work. Jesus foretold Peter's upcoming denial, which would reveal his true condition in contrast to what he'd imagined himself to be when he'd responded to Jesus earlier. "Peter said to Him, 'Lord, why can I not follow You right now? I will lay down my life for You.' Jesus answered, 'Will you lay down your life for Me? Truly, truly, I say to you, a rooster will not crow until you deny Me three times'" (John 13:27–28).

Sacrificial love, unselfish devotion, and a complete end of self are no more attainable by purely human means than is creating something from nothing. Man can no more become holy by some internal power than a leopard can change its spots (Jeremiah 13:23). Before a man can be made holy from within, he must be born anew, filled with the Spirit of the living God, and empowered by the very life of God Himself. What man needs above all else is the infusion of the life of God through the resurrection of Christ from the dead. It is the life of Christ that loves beyond all measure. Man does not possess love or selflessness, and neither does he think of others as more important than himself. Only when a man learns of his own wickedness because of sin—and Christ as the only source of God-centered goodness—can he say with the apostle Paul, "It is no longer I who live, but Christ lives in me."

Jesus understood perfectly what it takes to follow Him, and He knew that at the time of His death His disciples did not have it, and neither would they be faithful to Him. But their condition did not stop Him from loving them. In fact, their condition was the very reason He loved them the way He did. Jesus loved them by dying in their place so He could come again and fill them with His Holy Spirit. When Christ loved his disciples, He loved them perfectly, completely, without measure, and to the point of His own death. In this life, Jesus's disciples fail and falter, and they always will, and for this reason He left them promises of His own unfailing love. Perfectly true are the words of A. J. Flint:

> Though we may waver, He remains steadfast
> And all His words are sure;
> From everlasting unto everlasting
> His promises endure.
>
> Though we may wander, He will not forsake us,
> Truer than earthly friend;
> He never fails our trust, for having loved us,
> He loves unto the end.
>
> Unto the end; we doubt Him, we deny Him,
> We wound Him, we forget;
> We get some earthly idol up between us
> Without one faint regret.
>
> And when it falls or crumbles, and in anguish
> We seek this changeless Friend,
> Lo, He receives us, comforts and forgives us,
> And loves us to the end.

"Now before the Feast of the Passover, Jesus knowing that His hour had come that He would depart out of this world to the Father, having loved His own who were in the world, He loved them to the utmost" (John 13:1).

You need to know Jesus because He alone possesses the ideal love to comfort a sinner's ailing heart. Jesus alone can cleanse a defiled conscience, ease a sinner's mind when he feel like a failure, and restore a wayward soul. Jesus is the perfect comforter, because He does so with the selfless abandon of almighty God.

Within God Is a Heart
of Self-Denial

"Now before the Feast of the Passover, Jesus *knowing that His hour had come* that He would depart out of this world to the Father, having loved His own who were in the world, He loved them to the end." (John 13:1, emphasis added)

"Jesus spoke these things; and lifting up His eyes to heaven, He said, *'Father, the hour has come.'*" (John 17:1, emphasis added)

Jesus's Defining Hour:
Sacrificial Love and Infallible Justice That
Defined the World as Hopelessly Sinful

CHAPTER 6

JESUS'S DEFINING HOUR: THE DEFINITION OF GOD'S LOVE

"Now before the Feast of the Passover, Jesus *knowing that His hour had come* that He would depart out of this world to the Father, having loved His own who were in the world, He loved them to the end" (John 13:1, emphasis added).

Love can be expressed in many ways. There is puppy love between two children, and there is the selfish desire of two adults that masquerades as love. There is the obsession of a workaholic who tries to succeed at what he "loves," and there is also the willingness of a soldier to give his life for his comrades. There is always an admixture of selfish desire, self-sacrificing affection, and mere duty in all the ways men "love," because man cannot escape his sinful nature.

One thing that distinguishes Jesus from all other men is the way He loves. His love is perfectly pure as only God's love can be. His love is without measure and is given to those who can give Him nothing at all in return. Make no mistake: God derives pleasure from what He is accomplishing in some of His creatures. But God derives nothing good from men if He is not the cause. The cause of a pure, self-sacrificing love in men is the suffering of Christ.

The *Merriam-Webster Dictionary* defines *passion* as "the sufferings of Christ between the night of the Last Supper and his death." The reality of Jesus's love is never more clearly seen than during the period of time referred to as "His hour." Jesus had been teaching about the "hour" He would suffer and die. "And He began to teach them that the Son of Man must suffer many things and be rejected by the elders and the chief priests and the scribes, and be killed, and after three days rise again" (Mark 8:31).

The apostle John used the words "knowing that His hour had come" (John 13:1), which meant that the time of Jesus's suffering was at hand, and there would be no more waiting for it to occur. Furthermore, John wrote that Jesus began His high-priestly prayer (John 17:1) with the words, "Father, the hour has come," which marked the actual beginning of the hour following His prayer and entrance into His sufferings in Gethsemane. "The hour" refers to that distinct moment in time when God the Father looked upon God the Son as if He were responsible for the sins of men.

It is also important to understand that "the hour" is distinctly prophetic and is most clearly portrayed in two Old Testament traditions: (1) the Feast of Passover and (2) the sacrificial lamb. In chapter 13 John began by pointing to the Passover with the phrase "Now before the Feast of the Passover." The *Passover* refers to the death angel *passing over* each house where the blood of the sacrificial lamb was applied to the doorposts and beam (Exodus 12:13), which signified faith in God's promise that He would not kill the firstborn in the home where the blood was applied. It was during the feast of Passover that Jesus, the true sacrificial Lamb, offered Himself without spot or blemish (a picture of His being without sin) to appease God's anger toward idolatrous men (all who worship anything other than the one true God).

John stated before the Passover that Jesus loved His own and loved them to the end. This was a special time of Jesus' love. First, Jesus's love was special because of the comfort that He poured out upon His disciples during the hours prior to the cross. Second, it was special because of the cross itself, which was the greatest expression of self-sacrificing love the universe would ever behold. The scripture says that it was just prior to these events that Jesus knew "His hour" had come.

When John said, "That he would depart out of this world to the Father," he was speaking of Jesus's death, which was that of a condemned man. This "hour" referred to by John announced a pivotal point in history that was in fact the most significant hour of all time. Note that John said it was "His hour ... knowing that His hour had come." "The hour" was that period of time from His arrival in the garden of Gethsemane through the six hours He spent on the cross.

However, the last three hours Jesus spent on the cross were especially "His hour," because it was then that the Father poured out upon the Son the full penalty for man's sins. This period of time is exclusively and distinctly Jesus's hour, because what happened during that hour could only have been accomplished by Jesus Christ. This was the hour when God in Christ was going to fulfill all His promises to His people Israel and to the church. He would overcome the power of sin and death, reconcile a people to Himself, destroy the works of the devil, and fulfill to perfection His original design to make a people in His own image and after His likeness. This could not be done any other way with the same results, a point that I will prove in a later chapter.

What is especially important to emphasize at this point is that Jesus's love is so special because of the love He has for God the Father. Man is forever trying to make himself the center of everything, but he is not; God is. Jesus came to rectify man's condition before a holy God, but His primary motive was love for God the Father. Man's needs are second to God's. The God/man Christ Jesus loves the Father the way every man is meant to, and out of that kind of love He allowed Himself to be despised by the Father. Jesus's love is infinite, the Father's wrath is infinite, and at the cross infinite love met infinite wrath. With Jesus's love for the Father/God in view, John said that Jesus was going to depart out of this world *to the Father*; He was not departing to a *place* so much as to a *person*.

The apostle Paul stated that it was the Father's plan to send Jesus into the world: "Blessed be the God and Father of our Lord Jesus Christ, who has blessed us with every spiritual blessing in the heavenly places in Christ" (Ephesians 1:3). Jesus was fulfilling the Father's plan. It was for love of God the Father that God the Son bore the penalty of men in His own human body as He hung upon a cross, and it was to the Father that He now returned. Jesus loved the Father so much that He sacrificed Himself to please Him, and He replicated this love in His people through identification with them by becoming a human being. "For it was fitting that He, for whom and by whom all things exist, in bringing many sons to glory, should make the founder of their salvation perfect through suffering" (Hebrews 2:10). The love that God the Son has for God the Father is the very love that God imparts to His children through the sacrificial work of Christ.

Jesus's love is best defined by the degree to which He suffered in order to fulfill the Father's plan, which plan was to create a people made in His own image and to exalt for all time His Son in the process. Divine love is not defined by how much God gets but by how much He gave. At the cross Jesus gave it all, because it was there that the wrath of God was applied. So, in a way, the wrath of God defines the love of Christ, which was expressed during the time period we refer to as "His hour." We will look at the wrath of God and the "hour" that defines it from the words Jesus spoke in His high-priestly prayer in John 17:1.

In Jesus's prayer in this chapter, He was handing over His eleven remaining disciples to the Father to keep them from apostasy (falling away from the faith) during the time when He would not be able to intercede for them. Christ could not intercede for His own when He was bearing the guilt of their sin, so it became necessary for Jesus to hand over His disciples to the Father. Jesus said in His prayer, "Holy Father, keep them in Your name ... while I was with them, I was keeping them in Your name ... and I guarded them and not one of them perished ... But now I come to You."

Knowing that Jesus's *hour* was at hand, and that in His great high-priestly prayer He would hand over the guardianship of His disciples to the Father because He could not tend to it Himself while on the cross, God the Holy Spirit included a little phrase before the prayer as a footnote: "and lifting up His eyes to heaven." It is that footnote that God uses to express the love, sufferings, and wrath of God that are bound together during Jesus's *hour*.

Jesus's Hour Defined God's Wrath

John began his account of Jesus's high-priestly prayer in John 17:1 with these words: "And lifting up His eyes to heaven, He said, 'Father, the hour has come.'" It is not unusual for a person who is conscious of heaven as the abode of God to lift up his eyes to heaven when praying. Jesus lifting up His eyes to heaven is a beautiful picture when we consider the words from Psalms 14:2: "The LORD has looked down from heaven upon the sons of men to see if there are any who understand, who seek after God." From this verse we understand that God was looking down to earth to find someone seeking after Him, and in John 17:1 we are told that the incarnate Son of God was looking up toward heaven as He was about to utter the most striking prayer ever recorded in human history.

The concept is overwhelming, really, when we consider that as the Savior, the omnipresent God was reduced to a man on a vast planet that itself is infinitesimally small, like a speck in the vastness of an incomprehensible cosmos. Having become a man, the never-ending God found a way to express His love through infinite humility. As Jesus faced the cross, He looked into the night sky and beheld through human eyes the physical darkness. But in His spirit He faced the utmost darkness of all: He was to take the place of sinners and experience the wrath of God as it was unleashed upon Him.

Such a scene is recorded in Jesus's own words in Matthew 25:30: "Throw out the worthless slave into the outer darkness; in that place there will be weeping and gnashing of teeth." To be cast away from the loving presence of God is to be cast into outer darkness, as God is light and in Him there is no darkness at all (1 John 1:5); it is to be cast out of His favor, to be hated, abhorred, and despised by Him.

Furthermore, when God came down upon Mount Sinai at the giving of the law, He was present in the darkness. Darkness in one sense represents the judgment of God that comes upon all those who break His law (Exodus 20:21). What irony it is that Jesus, the eternal God who alone is worthy to be praised, should be treated in so worthless a way as to be thrown into the outer darkness, that place where there is weeping and gnashing of teeth. In contrast to this, there would be a day when a new song would be sung to this same Jesus: "Worthy is the lamb who was killed to receive power and wealth and wisdom and might and honor and glory and praise!" (Revelation 5:12).

But before that day could come, Jesus had to first endure the horrors of the crucifixion as He bore the punishment, penalty, and pain that our sin produced. Jesus dwelt in incomprehensible light and walked in the Father's love, and of Him we read, "This is my beloved Son, in whom I am well pleased." However, as the sin-bearer He would be cast into outer darkness far from His Father's favor. The Bible records His cry: "*Do not remain far away from me*, for trouble is near and I have no one to help me" (Psalms 22:11, emphasis added).

When there is no cloud cover, the evening sky is painted with twinkling little lights across the infinite, dark void. Each one of those tiny lights represents a solar star with enough radiant heat to reduce any planet to a burned-out cinder. However, at the correct distance of approximately ninety-three million miles, we can enjoy life on Earth because of the sun's life-giving rays. The night sky is filled with literally trillions of flickering little lights that represent an incomprehensible fiery force, which is a good picture of one of the twofold judgments of God upon a rebellious and depraved humanity. On the one hand, Christ was cast into outer darkness, and on the other, He was laid waste before the fiery wrath of almighty God. "Let us offer to God acceptable worship, with reverence and awe, for our God is a consuming fire" (Hebrews 12:28–29).

On that night so long ago, as Jesus looked up to heaven and before He prayed for Himself and for all His disciples, He stood on the very precipice of God's judgment on sin. Jesus was on His way to the garden of Gethsemane where He would sweat great drops of blood, and then He would endure the cross. He was facing His human inclinations to shrink back from the shame that would become His as He took the sinner's place of judgment before His heavenly Father. "Fixing our eyes on Jesus, the author and perfecter of faith, who for the joy set before Him endured the cross, *despising the shame,* and has sat down at the right hand of the throne of God" (Hebrews 12:2, emphasis added).

It is impossible for sinful men to conceive of the agony that Jesus felt on the cross, as He bore the full weight of sin's penalty under the Father's wrath. Sinful men do not live for God with their every thought, desire, attitude, and goal; they live for themselves. Sinful men do not desire the Father's good pleasure in what they do. Jesus alone lived exclusively for God, and when He died, He was severed from God's love and alienated from His favor.

When we look up at the night sky, we see twinkling little stars that press glimmering light through a black curtain. Before the Son of God looked into the very throne room of heaven where the mercy seat stood (Hebrews 9:24), which would soon accept His blood as a sacrificial offering for all the evils of men, He would first look intently upward toward a sky that was symbolically pregnant with foreboding judgment. Nevertheless, He did so with a passionate, unwavering, and perfect faith in God.

During "the hour" that defined Jesus, we see Him high and lifted up as the eternal sacrifice that properly defines true worship. In true worship there is an act of humble submission and obedience to the one true God of heaven. All the religions of the world exalt sinful men in an attempt to justify themselves, without any true acknowledgment of sin (Philippians 3). When Jesus died upon the cross, He defined God's wrath as the sin-bearer for God's justice. By contrast He also defined all forms of false and hypocritical religious worship.

Jesus's Hour Defined False Religious Worship

There was an hour, a moment in time, when Francis Scott Key stood in awe at what his eyes beheld, and his words recount his thoughts. "Oh, say, can you see, by the dawn's early light, what so proudly we hailed at the twilight's last gleaming? Whose broad stripes and bright stars, thru the perilous fight, o'er the ramparts we watched, were so gallantly streaming? And the rocket's red glare, the bombs bursting in air, gave proof through the night that our flag was still there. Oh, say does that star-spangled banner yet wave o'er the land of the free and the home of the brave?"

Francis Scott Key beheld uncommon valor as the men of Fort McHenry sustained bombardment throughout the night but would not surrender. Their character as they stood in harm's way was like a beacon of light to an act of bravery. Such men stand head and shoulders above those of us who have never had to face the brutality of war. There are countless memorable events in history that stand out far beyond the mundane occurrences of our normal lives. One event stands out infinitely further than all other unforgettable events, and Jesus made note of that particular moment when He said, "Father, the hour has come."

In history there have been countless men who have raised the flag of religious worship, but upon a closer look, we discover that most forms religion are false and based on pretention, self-justification, and hypocrisy. Jesus alone stands as a beacon of truth, for He sacrificed Himself (the innocent for the guilty) in the greatest act of heroism the universe will ever know. On the one hand, "the hour" defined Jesus by His sacrificial love and perfect religious worship of God the Father. And by way of contrast, "the hour" also defined all the forms of false religious worship. "Grace and *truth* came through Jesus Christ" (John 1), so all the religious forms that came before, and all the false Christs that have come after, are made manifest by looking at Jesus's defining hour.

The hour revealed all forms of false religious worship for what they truly are—rejection of the living God for personal gain and glory. "Pilate said to them, whom do you want me to release for you, Jesus Barabbas or Jesus who is Jesus called the Christ? (For he knew that they had handed him over because of envy)" (Matthew 27:17–18). Envy ruled the day for the religious leaders who sought the death of the Son of God. Those religious hypocrites used people for personal gain. They prospered financially and socially through self-aggrandizement at the cost of people's souls. Those religious leaders perfectly represented the false prophets of every age who lead a willing people astray.

The hour exposed Judas as the man who took the name *disciple* in vain and for personal gain. He never turned from his sin but instead, caring only for money, sold the Savior of men for thirty pieces of silver. "Now when Judas, who had betrayed him, saw that Jesus had been condemned, he regretted what he had done and returned the thirty silver coins to the chief priests and the elders, saying, 'I have sinned by betraying innocent blood!' But they said, 'What is that to us? You take care of it yourself!' So Judas threw the silver coins into the temple and left. Then he went out and hanged himself" (Matthew 27:3–5).

This was the hour that defined all human history, revealed God in all His glory, and man in all his moral depravity; love never loomed so bright, self-sacrifice so sweet, the meaning behind human existence so clear, and the wickedness of men as dark as during that hour.

Jesus's hour revealed just how great a sin it is to make idols of stone. The religious elite of Jesus's day cared so much for the temple as a place of worship that they forbade certain categories of people from entering in.

God, however, cares more for people than He does for objects of stone. At the same time that the religious leaders were forbidding people they regarded as unqualified to worship God to enter the temple, they were permitting greed and thievery to take place within its walls.

After making a scourge and chasing false worshippers from God's house, Jesus responded to their hypocrisy and greed with these words: "Take these things away; stop making My Father's house a place of business" (John 2:16).

The religious leaders responded by saying, "What sign do You show us as your authority for doing these things?"

Jesus responded to their inquiry by saying, "Destroy this temple, and in three days I will raise it up."

The religious leaders were so fixed on the building they worshipped in—and misused—that they missed the true Temple who was standing before them, reproving them of their misdeeds and loving them by doing so. They worshipped the temple of stone but hated the true temple of God's body in Jesus Christ. In God's desire to finish what He'd started at creation, He prepared a body for Christ, and so it is written, "Therefore, when He comes into the world, He says, 'Sacrifice and offering You have not desired, But a body You have prepared for Me'" (Hebrews 10:5). Jesus's hour revealed to the world that it is all too possible to raise a great edifice to worship a false god while seeking to destroy the true One.

Jesus's hour revealed that taking the Lord's name in vain (acting as a follower of Christ when you're not) is a hypocritical act to cover what actually exists in one's own heart, which is a hatred for the Lord's Christ. Judas regretted his actions on a human level, but he did not repent in an acceptable way before God. That is, he did not turn from sin to God (1 Thessalonians 1:9). It was a purely selfish act of remorse that caused him to go out and hang himself. His betrayal of Christ showed that his heart was devoid of the spiritual life of God. Judas represents people of every age who take the name of the Lord in vain without any internal reality.

"(Now this man Judas acquired a field with the reward of his unjust deed, and falling headfirst he burst open in the middle and all his intestines gushed out. This became known to all who lived in Jerusalem, so that in their own language they called that field Hakeldama, that is, 'Field of Blood.')" (Acts 1:18–19).

The hour revealed man's insatiable desire to rule his own life and his unwillingness to be told how he should live or to be held accountable for the same. As a result of man's desire to be in the place of God, all men call for Jesus's death. "Pilate said to them, 'Then what should I do with Jesus who is called the Christ?' They all said, 'Crucify him!' He asked, 'Why? What wrong has he done?' But they shouted more insistently, 'Crucify him!'" (Matthew 29:32–33).

So it is with men today. They are all too willing to place guilt upon God, who is innocent. Men believe that all the evil in the world is God's fault, whether they say it directly or not. Men believe in God's guilt without any evidence that He has done anything wrong. Singer and songwriter Gilbert O'Sullivan put it this way. "Reality came around, And without so much as a mere touch, Cut me into little pieces, Leaving me to doubt Talk about, God in His mercy, Oh, if he really does exist, Why did he desert me."

I have nothing against the songwriter personally, but in his thinking, God is deserting him rather than the other way around. God has cursed man as a result of man's giving into the devil's lies, which accuse God of the very thing that man is all too willing to propose: that God is unjust and responsible for all the evil in the world. Mankind has always been willing to place upon God the evils that men have produced and for which they are responsible. Sinful men feel more comfortable making God responsible for evil than themselves. They deny His existence by disobedience and selfish and immoral behavior, and they do these things with no fear of His just judgment. If men could or would obey God, the result would be a perfectly peaceful and harmonious world.

Man rejects the light that God provides in the person of Jesus Christ, and he acts as if he could do better if only he were in charge. A song by Pete Seeger and Lee Hays, written in 1949, says, "If I had a hammer ... I'd hammer out danger, I'd hammer out a warning, and I'd hammer out love between my brothers and my sisters, all over this land." At the time of Jesus's death, one man did have a hammer—a Roman soldier and representative of the human race who nailed love incarnate to a wooden cross. What that Roman soldier did in ignorance men now do in full light of the gospel's truth.

We all live in ignorance until the good news of God's love is revealed to us. When the truth is declared to us, we still continue in our rebellious manner of life until—if God chooses—His mighty hand performs a miracle and transforms our stony heart so that we receive the provision of His Son. Pilate tried to absolve himself of responsibility from Jesus's unjust death by washing his hands with water. However, it takes more than water to wash oneself from the guilt of Jesus's blood. Ironically, it takes the blood of Christ—that is, His sacrificial death.

Furthermore, Jesus's hour revealed the true nature of sabbath-breaking. God set apart the sabbath as a day to worship Him (Exodus 20), but as previously stated, men do not regard God as separate and set apart from the rest of His creation. Instead God receives man's scorn. This can easily be seen when men use the name of Jesus Christ as a swear word, but most times men conceal their scorn with much hypocrisy. In our generation, however, that hypocrisy has begun to disappear in view of a more straightforward denial of God. Jesus fulfilled the Sabbath when, by His sacrificial death, He set apart men who could worship the Father in spirit and in truth. Because of the sin of Sabbath-breaking all the evils of suffering, disease, sickness, and death were heaped upon God the Son instead of sinful men.

"'You have heard the blasphemy! What is your verdict?' They all condemned him as deserving death. Then some began to spit on him, and to blindfold him, and to strike him with their fists, saying, 'Prophesy!' The guards also took him and beat him. They began to salute him: 'Hail, king of the Jews!' Again and again they struck him on the head with a staff and spit on him. Then they knelt down and paid homage to him" (Mark 14:64–65; 15:18–19).

The hour of which Jesus spoke revealed with perfect clarity the evils hidden in men's hearts, which are covered by deceitful words, dishonest associations, untrustworthy acts of "worship," and fraudulent deeds of benevolence. It is no coincidence that the men who engineered Jesus's death as a criminal—which they did out of jealousy—were among the most fastidiously religious people in all of history. Jesus Christ was mistreated, misunderstood, and rejected because of self-centered pride and resentment toward the sovereign God of the universe. Like a planet darkened by the blackness of space, so is the human heart blinded by ignorance of God's wrath toward sin, which was emptied on His beloved Son for sinners. This was the hour of which Christ spoke.

Jesus's Hour Defined God's Sacrificial Love

"Having loved His own that were in the world, He loved them to the utmost." (John 13:1)

Jesus, who loves the Father with an eternal and infinite love, and who sacrificed Himself completely for the Father's good pleasure, also loved those in the world, and he loved them to the utmost. The cross is not simply an event in human history; it is also a characteristic of self-denial that is found at the very core of the triune God. We can better understand this concept if we look at the relationship between each of the persons of the Godhead.

The Father planned and purposed to exalt the Son before all creation, to make Him the central figure in all things, and to glorify Him throughout all eternity. The Son, in perfect acknowledgment of the Father's will, submitted to His desires and purpose in the greatest act of suffering and self-denial that the world will ever behold. The Holy Spirit quietly works in creation and cares for believers as their intercessor, and yet He makes a minimal declaration of His person and work as mighty God, equal with the Father and the Son in Holy Scripture. The triune God is truly, in all His perfection, a self-denying God in reference to the other persons of the Trinity. It is the love within the Trinity that governs the love of God toward His creation.

The world defines love primarily as something we receive. God defines it as something He gives. "For God so loved the world that *He gave* His only begotten Son" (John 3:16, emphasis added). In order for God to give love on His terms, He had to be willing to deny Himself. Self-denial is the way God defines love. Divine love cost God the Father His beloved Son, because during Jesus's hour the Father placed upon Him the eternal punishment of sin. "He who knew no sin became sin on our behalf..." (1 Cor. 5:21). God the Father—who brought forth His Son eternally, loved Him perfectly, and has been well pleased with Him—placed upon Him an eternal payment for man's wickedness. That is self-denying love!

The Son's self-denying love was also on display as He bore the separation from the Father for the sake of those He loved. God's love cost the Son His rightful place in the created order. "Being found in appearance as a man, He humbled Himself by becoming obedient to the point of death, even death on a cross" (Philippians 2:8). He who is infinite in all ways became a finite man and, even worse, a substitute for evil. That is self-denying love. During Jesus's hour, self-denial was on display like at no other time in human history. God became a man for this very purpose:

JOE DURSO

to bear the sins of many. He appeased the righteousness of God, and He became a uniquely divine and human substitute. Christ did all of that, first and foremost, for the Father's good pleasure and glory, but He also did it for those for whom He died, and that is self-denying love.

The self-denying love of Christ is incomprehensible when you really stop to think about it. By virtue of His divine nature, God is omnipotent, and yet Christ, in becoming a man, offered up prayers—supplications with crying and tears—asking to be saved. "In the days of His flesh, he offered up both prayers and supplications with loud crying and tears to the One able to save Him from death, and He was heard because of His piety" (Hebrews 5:7). That is self-abasement and self-denying love. By virtue of His divine nature, God knows all things, and yet Christ, in becoming a man, learned obedience from what He suffered. "Although He was a Son, He learned obedience from the things which He suffered" (Hebrews 5:8). That is self-abasement and self-denying love.

We live in a world that is crazy about power. What kind of power does it take to forgive those who nail you to a piece of wood, stick it in the ground, and make a joke of you when they do it? What strength of character must a person possess to forgive those who are in the processes of murdering him? Consider the character of soul that beat within the heart of Christ as He was derided, scorned, and mocked before and during His death by crucifixion. "But Jesus was saying, 'Father, forgive them; for they do not know what they are doing.' And they cast lots, dividing up His garments among themselves" (Luke 23:34).

So, then, who was Jesus speaking of when He cried for the forgiveness of His persecutors? Did Jesus ask forgiveness for those He knew would reject His substitutionary death? According to Jesus's words in John 17:9, He did not. There He prayed specifically to the Father, "I do not ask on behalf of the world but for those whom you have given me." Were Jesus's words partial toward those chosen by the Father, and did He at that time reject those who had rejected Him? It is important to understand that there are two distinct natures operating in the Messiah (Savior) of God. He is distinctly God and distinctly man. As God, Jesus loves the world, but because He placed an element of freedom within man, man became responsible for his moral choices. Therefore, as God, Jesus must judge mankind justly.

82

But did Jesus judge men when He was on the cross? It is important to understand that as a man Jesus loved those who treated Him with the utmost disdain and cruelty, without personal malice and selfish jealousy. Jesus the man did not take matters into His own hands. He did not interfere with the Father's plan outwardly or within His soul. He did not take personal revenge. Perfect justice was reserved for a time yet future by Jesus, the eternal Son.

By nature, all men reject the existence of God, which was portrayed perfectly in the denial and death of the Christ by those who should have received Him most gladly in light of a three-year ministry that healed their nation. Jesus healed individuals from all kinds of diseases, fed them with food, and even raised the dead. However, there was no personal revenge in the heart of Jesus the man. He could say with perfect transparency and accuracy, "Father, forgive them; for they do not know what they are doing."

Jesus, the Son of God, does not act according to personal revenge either. However, He is propelled but an infinite and perfect sense of justice. In fact, He is the source of justice. Jesus does not received justice from any outside source the way we do; He is the very origin of justice. The eternal God operates in a way completely different from the way we operate, which is why He is holy and in need of nothing. The Son of God shone through Jesus the man, who acted in a way consistent with His position as the second person of the divine Trinity. He never took matters into His own hands but committed Himself to the Father by word and deed, all the way to the depths of His human soul.

How then do we react to the generosity of Jesus's character of soul in light of the injustice and cruelty that was perpetrated upon Him? Do we recognize the poverty of our own souls in light of His magnanimity? Do we bow before Him in utter disgust for our own petty and inflated pride that ignores His sacrifice and sufferings? Have we been so touched by the magnitude of His love that we lay prostrated upon the ground and beg Him to receive our cries for divine mercy?

It is the desire of the author of this book that if you have not already seen your need for unnatural humility, you would bow before Jesus as the beggar that we all are and cry for His divine aid. I pray that you would see Jesus as God, the only Savior, and the only one who can save your soul. I desire that you would cry out to Him to save you.

WITHIN GOD IS A HEART OF SELF-SACRIFICING LOVE

"He made Him who knew no sin to be sin on our behalf, so that we might become the righteousness of God in Him." (2 Corinthians 5:21)

When Absolute Purity Became Sin

CHAPTER 7

JESUS'S SACRIFICIAL DEATH:
THE COST OF GOD'S LOVE

Many years ago I was speaking to a fellow worker about abortion. At first he argued in defense of a woman's right to choose, but suddenly he stopped and said, "Joe, I am not saying it is right to have an abortion." Then he wiped a tear from his eye. He was a very unlikely man to do this. He was macho, self-assured, and even arrogant, at least at times. Nevertheless, he pulled a piece of paper from his wallet as he continued. "Some years ago an ex-girlfriend decided to have an abortion without telling me first." He then proceeded to read a poem he'd written after realizing he'd lost a child that he would never get to know—at least in this lifetime. Then *I* wanted to cry.

The Christian understands the suffering that is in the world: the countless young mothers who lose their newborn infants, the soft-hearted individuals betrayed by lifelong best friends, the family members and friends who have lost loved ones to war, the men who have spent a lifetime building businesses only to have them stolen by thieves, the people treated like outcasts because of their nationality, and the children left without parents for numerous reason. These and many other scenarios paint the picture of suffering in our present world, and such suffering is common to all mankind.

What unregenerate men do not understand and are unwilling to understand is the fact that all the suffering in the world is a consequence of their sin. God has built suffering into this present world as a result of consequences produced by sin, in order that men might become guilty before Him in their own minds and consciences. However, read a book or listen to the news, and you will quickly realize that man does not endorse the notion of sin. He takes no personal responsibility for evil in the world, and he will stand firm on the notion that men begin good from birth. Such refusal to believe the inherent evil that exists in all men is completely and diametrically opposed to the teaching of scripture, which recounts man as evil and deserving of all the consequences that this present world can produce.

The Guilt All Men Accumulate

Since the beginning of human history there has not been one person who has not committed evil of one kind or another. Everyone has been guilty of at least one of the following wrongdoings. Everyone has envied the success of others, failed to forgive the misdoings of others, failed to give proper honor to God for this present creation, become enslaved to idolatrous passions, falsely professed an intimate knowledge of God, disrespected the sabbath, disrespected his parents, desired someone other than his spouse, stolen, or lied about someone else. The previous list is abbreviated and far from exhaustive. There are no perfect people, and all of them—if they are honest with themselves and others—would readily admit that their lives are full of regrets for poor behavior. Everyone sins. "For all have sinned and fall short of the glory of God" (Romans 3:23), or so says the scripture. God tells us forcefully and directly that all men sin.

> *There is none righteous, not even one;* there is none who understands, there is none who seeks for God; all have turned aside, together they have become useless; there is none who does good, there is not even one. Their throat is an open grave, with their tongues they keep deceiving, the poison of asps is under their lips; whose mouth is full of cursing and bitterness; their feet are swift to shed blood, destruction and misery are in their paths, and the path of peace they have not known. There is no fear of God before their eyes. (Romans 3:10–18, emphasis added)

There are none who are perfect and without sin according to God's standards—except one person. He was the only begotten and beloved Son of God who suffered all the consequences of a wrathful God, and He did so while being guilty of no wrongdoing. No man has ever suffered the wrath of God on sin in this life, only sin's consequences. Jesus alone suffered the wages of sin while He hung upon the cross. Consequences help sinful men to see the evil that is in sin, but it is not evil itself. A man drinks too much wine, falls down drunk on a railroad track, and loses his legs. That tragedy is the consequence of sin, not the evil of it. A man forces a woman to lie with him, and as a result she bears the emotional pain and suffering of having been used in a shameful and demeaning way for the rest of her life. That suffering is the consequence of sin but not the evil of it. Many such examples can be given, and in every case the consequences point to the evil of sin, but they are not the sin itself.

> Man is not a sinner because he sins; he sins because he is a sinner.

The evil of sin has to do with the motive behind the thought, will, word, and action. *Man is not a sinner because he sins; he sins because he is a sinner.* The primary motive behind every sin is human pride that exalts man above God and rebels against the knowledge of Him. In contrast to sinful men who exalt themselves above God, there is Jesus who, being God, humbled Himself by becoming a man.

The character of Jesus is revealed in this scripture: "Have this attitude in yourselves which was also in Christ Jesus, who, although He existed in the form of God, did not regard equality with God a thing to be grasped, but emptied Himself, taking the form of a slave, and being made in the likeness of men. Being found in appearance as a man, He humbled Himself by becoming obedient to the point of death, even death on a cross" (Philippians 2:5–8).

The state of evil is selfish, self-seeking, and self-absorbed, and the best of men cannot avoid the presence of these traits residing in their hearts. Just ask the spouse of any person if this is so. The state of evil is unconscious of the needs, cares, and concerns of others and especially of God, and it abounds greatly with regard to God. Jesus views sin as infinitely and intensely evil because of the selfish nature of it, which means that the person who sins is uncaring about the existence of God. The apostle Paul, when writing about the state of the sinner, penned these words: "And just as they did not see fit to acknowledge God any longer" (Romans 1:28). The nature of sinful man is contrary to the first and great command of God, which is to love God with all our mind, heart, soul, and strength. Love is unselfish, and it seeks not its own, according to 1 Corinthians 13.

Evil is the opposite of love. It is filled with hate and contempt for others, which sometimes is manifest simply by indifference. Fallen men are contrary to God because God is good and we are evil. God is love and thereby unselfish, understanding, kind, patient, and merciful—and thereby good. But men are hateful and thereby selfish, unkind, impatient, and unmerciful—and thereby evil. Evil men do not view God in his appropriate place, which is at the center of all things. They ignore God and fail to even acknowledge His presence. Jesus hates evil because the evil person does not acknowledge the one true and infinitely holy God.

The Penalty Jesus Endured

There is a clear contrast in scripture between the way men view sin and the way God does. As men of a fallen and sinful race, our view of sin is skewed, and we fail to see it for what it truly is. We are born in sin: we enjoy it, indulge in it, and desire it, and at times we are completely unaware of it. We forget our sins, love them, and at times suffer with a guilty conscience because of them. Yet we remain indifferent to them. Jesus was born of a virgin and of the seed of His heavenly Father. He is holy, undefiled, and separate from sinners (Hebrews 7:26), and therefore He does not share our sinful condition.

Furthermore, Jesus is equal with God in every way because He is God. The holy Trinity—or three distinct persons in one God—are beyond human comprehension, but the concept is understandable and reasonable. The Trinitarian teaching does not say that there are three Gods and, at the same time, one God; that would be unreasonable. However, it does say that there are three persons in one God, which is perfectly reasonable. Jesus is the second person of the Trinity and is equal with God in every way. Jesus is fully God and fully human. When I say that Jesus is of the seed of His

Father, I mean that He is of the same essence as God the Father because He came from the Father. Jesus came from the Father into time when He became a man. He came from the Father, being eternal or outside of time. I say all of that in order to make the point that Jesus is characterized by all that God is, as revealed in the Bible, which includes His awareness and hatred of sin.

We say that Jesus is of the same essence as the Father because He came from the Father, and this He did in a way that is different from all other created beings. Jesus came from the Father in the same way my son came forth from me. My son is fully human; he possesses all the characteristics of one who is human. My son is fully human because he came from me and I am fully human. All things were created by God out of nothing. The human race did not come forth from God. If it had, then we would be of the same essence as God, and we would be God. Only Christ came forth from the Father eternally, and therefore He is one with God, and He is God. Because Jesus is God in human flesh, He also possesses all the characteristics of God.

The distance between Jesus's understanding of evil and our own is so great that it could be compared to the distance between the infinite universe and us. Jesus abhors it completely. The best that finite men can hope to understand is the concept of infinite love, but Jesus has a full understanding in an eternal experience with God the Father and the Holy Spirit. The best we can hope for is to understand the concept of a sinful heart that seeks to overthrow the sovereign rule of almighty God. But Jesus, with perfect and experiential clarity, saw sin exactly for what it is, and He went to the cross anyway. That is infinite love! Jesus took to Himself the full consciousness and guilt of our sins as the Father poured out upon Him the due penalty of those sins, and He held nothing back. Jesus, with full understanding of sin's evil, absorbed God's full and infinite hatred of that sinful evil.

When Jesus took to Himself the guilt and presence of sin in our place, He did so with exactly the same disdain and aversion that the one true God has for it. We are told that Jesus's agony began in a garden called Gethsemane, for that was where the Father began to withdraw from Him. "And being in agony He was praying very fervently; and His sweat became like drops of blood, falling down upon the ground" (Luke

22:44). The agony that Jesus endured in the garden of Gethsemane was not a common reaction of men to their sin. In that passage we are given a picture of Christ's agony as life-giving rain falling to the ground. It was the rain of God's holiness and utter contempt for all that is wicked that brought His tears to the ground, and this pictures for us the coming of life and purification of our hearts, if we come to believe in Jesus.

Understand that during the last three hours Jesus spent upon the cross, He absorbed an eternal punishment for our sin, because the penalty of our sin is an eternal one, "If your eye causes you to stumble, throw it out; it is better for you to enter the kingdom of God with one eye, than, having two eyes, to be cast into hell, where their worm does not die, and the fire is not quenched" (Mark 9:47–48).

"And the smoke of their torment goes up forever and ever; they have no rest day and night, those who worship the beast and his image, and whoever receives the mark of his name" (Revelation 14:11).

"And the devil who deceived them was thrown into the lake of fire and brimstone, where the beast and the false prophet are also; and they will be tormented day and night forever and ever" (Revelation 20:10).

The man who sins against finite man receives the penalty of death, which is the separation from this present and temporal life. The man who sins against the eternal God receives eternal punishment. We cannot even begin to conceive of the sufferings of Christ as He bore in His body the eternal penalty for each and every person's sin for whom He died. Jesus died for each and every person throughout the entire world, and for every generation from Adam until the end of human history. Not one sin was missed; not one overlooked; and not one was hated insufficiently to punish. God knew them all, just as He has all the hairs of our head numbered, and as He has a name for every star in the heavens, which are as the sand on the seashore (Psalms 147:4). God has knowledge of a trillion cells in all six billion people who live in our present world. Even so, the Holy Spirit has knowledge of each and every sin of each and every person since the beginning of time, and He poured out the entire penalty for all of those sins on the Son of God with a Holy vengeance.

It is at this point that the cults, those imitators of Christianity, go the most seriously wrong, because they do not acknowledge Christ as the one, true, and infinite God. Instead they reduce Him to a mere man and created being. However, a created and finite being could not endure an eternal punishment in three hours. Nor does such a one have the righteousness necessary to satisfy God. It takes the infinite to reach into eternity and pay the price for an infinite transgression. Furthermore, it takes the inherent goodness of the self-existent God to pay the rightful price for such a transgression. If an angel without sin were to die for the sins of one man, he could not do it rightfully, because the righteousness of the angel is an imparted righteousness received from a holy God. God alone is the eternal I AM, and as such all things come from Him, and without Him nothing can exist— including righteousness. An angel can receive the righteousness that God bestows, but he cannot bestow a righteousness that is not inherently his own. God is the source of all righteousness, and He alone can bestow it. One of His names proclaims Him to be "the Lord our Righteousness" (Jeremiah 23:6; 1 Corinthians 1:30).

Let us consider the way God imparts divine truth as a way to understand how He must impart His righteousness. Men can speak divine truth in the hearing of other men, and we call that teaching, and it is. But in reality, only God can impart divine revelation. It is the work of God the Holy Spirit to take divine truth (truth that originates in God) and make it known to whom He wills (Romans 8:16; 1 John 2:27). Jesus made it clear that God alone is the true dispenser of knowledge when He taught the oneness of God in Matthew 23:8–10: "But do not be called Rabbi; for One is your Teacher, and you are all brothers. Do not call anyone on earth your father; for One is your Father, He who is in heaven. Do not be called leaders; for One is your Leader, that is, Christ."

Jesus taught that human teachers are merely conduits by which God imparts divine truth. Three terms that men are not call other men, as translated from the Greek, refer to a person of honor, an imparter of knowledge, and a master or teacher. Jesus said that no man is to be called *rabbi* or *leader*, and that no one should call another man *father*. It is not the act of calling someone by those titles that is the focus of Jesus's attention but the belief that a person could have abilities that belong to God alone. Truly, there is only one person of honor, imparter of knowledge, and master—and that is God, omnipotent and omniscient, the Father and source of all things. To make this even clearer, the words used in the verses 8–10 are not all the same. The word for *rabbi* refers to a person of honor, but the second word in the phrase "for *One* is your Teacher" is the word from which we get the English word *doctor* or *expert*. Only God is all-knowing, and only in Him does truth reside inherently. In same way that only God can impart knowledge, only God can impart righteousness.

Unlike the teaching scenario, there can be no conduit for paying the price of sin and imparting divine righteousness, because that particular transaction is beyond the ability of the creature to even be used as such. In the area of a sacrifice, it is a life for a life, or an innocent person for a guilty person. We have already showed that there is no innocent person but all are guilty. Therefore, God had to become a man in order that He might take the blame, pay the penalty, and impart His righteousness to the sinner's account.

And for whom did Jesus die? Surely it was not for those who will pay the price for their own sins throughout all eternity. Rather, it is for those of us—the elect—who have trusted in Jesus Christ alone for our salvation and have been forgiven by His unmerited favor. It was our sins that put Him there, but it was not our sins that kept Him there. Neither was it Roman nails that bound Jesus to the torment of Calvary. Christ was kept on the cross by His own love for the Father and His plan of salvation.

The year was 1975, and I was working for a company that installed garage doors. I swung the claws of my hammer in an attempt to remove a hinge from a door that needed to be replaced, and suddenly blood shot out of my arm to about five feet. I dropped the hammer and grabbed my arm in an attempt to stop the bleeding. At first I was stunned by what had happened, but later an X-ray revealed that a fragment from a cast-iron hinge (the size of a twenty-two-caliber bullet) had broken off and hit me in the arm.

During those years I went to the emergency room many times, so I know what it is to get stitches and to be shot up with painkillers. However, on this particular day I felt everything the ER doctor did. I heard one doctor tell the other, "Make it a little bigger." "It" was the size of the incision through which they got at the fragment. I heard and felt the scissors they used, the probing for the piece of metal, and its extraction. The pain started in my forearm and radiated all the way to my shoulder. During that time I quoted Psalms 62:6 to myself many times: "He only [is] my rock and my salvation: [he is] my defense; I shall not be moved."

However, I could feel within myself some anger toward the two men who were trying their best to help me, though they had no part in the reason for my suffering. I don't know why the pain medicine had no effect, but I do know that during the surgery Jesus was my rock and my refuge.

However, Jesus literally suffered infinitely more, not physically but emotionally and spiritually by the will and power of a holy God. Jesus had nowhere to turn for comfort, because the only one who could comfort Him (God) was the very one who was causing His suffering as He rectified all our wrongdoing. At a human level, the men who placed Him on the instrument of His human death were, by representation, the very ones who had caused His suffering, as He was the sacrificial Lamb.

What strength of character does it take to restrain one's sense of justice? For there was no justice at that moment for Jesus, only a substitution of His submission and righteousness for our rebellion and sin. His sense of justice should have told Him, "No, I am not guilty," and then it would have turned His anger upon the guilty ones. But it was not justice that Jesus felt in that hour; it was love and forgiveness. At the very time that man nailed Him to a piece of wood, He said, "Father, forgive them for they know not what they do." We all understand what it is to have our toes stepped on, to experience wrongdoing by others, to feel rejection when we are overlooked, mistreated, or even used wrongfully as a means of lifting someone else up. Jesus, however, experienced such things and much more as coming from every person who has ever or will ever live. And He did so at the very moment that God took out—on Jesus—His anger against our sin.

When we think of Jesus's character, we should consider the strength of love it took to restrain an infinite sense of justice in the face of sinful injustice, an infinite sense of outrage in the face of selfishness, pride, and callousness found in the human heart. Take whatever pain you have ever experienced and understand that Jesus's pain took Him into eternity future in order to pay its price, and He did so out of love in the midst of complete injustice.

The Righteousness Jesus Imputed

Christ alone was the spotless Lamb who could take away the sins of men. "Knowing that you were not redeemed with perishable things like silver or gold from your futile way of life inherited from your forefathers, but with precious blood, as of a lamb unblemished and spotless, the blood of Christ" (1 Peter 1:18–19).

John the Baptist confirmed the same idea in John 1:36: "And he looked at Jesus as He walked, and said, "Behold, the Lamb of God!" Repeated often are the Bible's admonitions that the sacrificial lamb to be offered by the people was to be spotless. All such declarations pointed to the Messianic Lamb who was to pay for the sins of men. Animals, spotless though they may be, cannot take away the blemish of sins from men. "For it is impossible for the blood of bulls and goats to take away sins" (Hebrews 1:4), because only a man can die to take away the sins of a man. Bulls and goats were only meant to be a picture pointing to Christ.

We are told in 2 Corinthians 5:21 that our standing as righteous before God is tightly tied to Jesus, who first took our guilt upon Him. "He made Him who knew no sin to be sin on our behalf, so that we might become the righteousness of God in Him." Only when our guilt was removed in the sight of God through the sufferings and death of Christ could His righteousness be applied to us.

Righteousness, by definition in the Greek, is integrity, virtue, purity of life, rightness, and correctness of thinking, feeling, and acting. It was at the cross of Calvary in history past that the penalty of sin rested on Christ so that His righteousness could be applied to the saint. In the present, the same transaction takes place in the heart of the individual believer. The proof that Jesus Christ was completely righteous was demonstrated in His resurrection from the dead.

One of the clearest statements in the Bible concerning Jesus's person as being God in the flesh is found in (Romans 1:4): "Who was declared the Son of God with power by the resurrection from the dead, according to the Spirit of holiness, Jesus Christ our Lord." This statement declaring Jesus to be God comes right on the heels of verse 3, which declares Him to be the Son of man: "Concerning His Son, who was born of a descendant of David according to the flesh." The phrase "His Son" refers back to verse 1, which says, "Paul, a slave of Christ Jesus, called as an apostle, set apart for the gospel of God." So, when Paul said "His Son," he was referring back to the gospel of God, which meant that Jesus was the Son of God.

In verse 4 Paul said that Jesus was declared to be the Son of God, which declaration was made with power by the resurrection from the dead. The power that Paul was referring to was the power it took to raise Jesus from the dead. Why power? According to Romans 6:23, "The wages of sin is death." People die as a consequence of sin, which is according to the will of God. God is eternal, so the penalty is eternal; to be removed from the eternal penalty would take a reversal of the ordained will of God. The soul that sins must die (Ezekiel 18:4).

We must then answer the question: what would it take for God to reverse His decision? In Romans 1:4 we are given the answer: the power of the Jesus's resurrection, which was "according to the Spirit of holiness." Jesus lived a sinless and perfectly holy life for some thirty-three years. Therefore, sin could not hold Him in the grave. He died on behalf of guilty men and not His own sin. When Jesus was resurrected from the dead, it proved that He had fully paid the eternal price for those for whom He'd died. When Jesus was resurrected from the dead, He also brought up from the grave with Him all those for whom He had died—not physically, because many had not even been born yet, but judicially.

The Bible makes it abundantly clear that righteousness is given to men on the basis of faith, as a gift, not as a result of good works. "Because by the works of the Law no flesh will be justified in His sight; for through the Law comes the knowledge of sin" (Romans 3:20). "But now apart from the Law the righteousness of God has been manifested, being witnessed by the Law and the Prophets," (Romans 3:21). "For the demonstration, I say, of His righteousness at the present time, so that He would be just and the justifier of the one who has faith in Jesus" (Romans 3:26). "For we maintain that a man is justified by faith apart from works of the Law" (Romans 3:28).

Many more verses could be cited that declare righteousness as a free gift of God's grace. The sin that men accumulate to their account in the course of a lifetime is so great that no amount of good works could possibly undo the pending consequences. Each sin that a man commits carries with it an eternal penalty of punishment.

The doctrine of imputation is completely contrary to salvation by works. Imputation is that means of salvation by which God places to the sinner's account His own righteousness, a doctrine that is stated as early as the book of Genesis. In Genesis 15 God made a covenant with Abraham and promised him that his descendants would be like the stars in the sky. "Then he believed in the Lord; and He reckoned it to him as righteousness" (Genesis 15:6). The doctrine of imputation declares that righteousness is not man's inherently but as a result of a gift received from God. The doctrine of justification declares that man is made just in God's sight by the gift of God's Son who washed away the penalty of man's sins. Imputation and justification are two pieces of salvation by grace alone. It might be said that *justification*, like *imputation*, are on the same side of a single coin. On the opposite side of that coin is *sanctification*.

Sanctification is the means by which God imparts His own righteous life into the soul of the believer so that the believer might experience the life of God. God is said to be holy, which means He is separate from the rest of His creation. The term is taken from a Hebrew concept found in the word *ko'-desh*, which means "to be separate or set apart." God is separate by means of His inherent characteristics, which are infinite and eternal in every way. Man is created in time and is limited in every way. When the Bible says that man is holy, or is to be holy, it means that man is to be set apart to God, who is intrinsically holy. Man is made holy through sanctification.

The Resurrection Jesus Imparts

Salvation can never be through works that proceed from an intrinsically evil heart. Jesus said, "For from within, out of the heart of men, proceed the evil thoughts, fornications, thefts, murders, adulteries" (Mark 7:21). Evil proceeds from an evil heart.

The Bible speaks about the evils of men, and it also speaks about the good. "There will be tribulation and distress for every soul of man who does evil, of the Jew first and also of the Greek, but glory and honor and peace to everyone who does good" (Romans 2:9–10).

When the Bible speaks about the good that men do, it is not speaking about an intrinsic good, as if the man were born good, but about the good that results from a changed and repentant heart—a new creation, which is the work of God. "Therefore if anyone is in Christ, he is a new creature; the old things passed away; behold, new things have come" (2 Corinthians 5:17).

"Do not lie to one another since you have put off the old man with its practices and have been clothed with the new man that is being renewed in knowledge according to the image of the one who created it" (Colossians 3: 9–10).

"You were taught with reference to your former way of life to lay aside the old man who is being corrupted in accordance with deceitful desires, to be renewed in the spirit of your mind, and to put on the new man who has been created in God's image—in righteousness and holiness that comes from truth" (Ephesians 4:2–24).

After Jesus died, He was buried; and after three days He was raised from the dead with power. The life that came up from the dead was the intrinsic life of Christ that could not be held in the grave by sin, because He died for a sin that was not His own. The resurrected life of Christ is the new life that is imparted into the believer's soul.

There is only one correct response for such an unspeakable gift of forgiveness and imparted righteousness, and that is complete and unending gratitude. We do not seek to do right because we want to repay God for giving us eternal life, a holy and moral will, and a secure existence in which goodness, peace, joy, and contentment reign in our hearts continually. But we live solely and completely out of gratitude. Right living should be exalted in our minds so that doing what is right is the only thing we consider doing—as soon as we realize what the right thing is. Study of scripture then becomes a number-one priority, because only in the Bible can we learn how to do the right thing.

Righteousness never exists in a vacuum. Righteous living always includes service to the God who created us and cares for all the other people He created as well. We should always view righteous living as the way we treat and respond to the almighty God above—and all the people who live alongside us here on earth. How then shall we live? By faith in a promise-keeping God who forgives our sins if we repent and then bids us do the same for our fellow man.

During the writing of this book I was privileged to appreciate more deeply how meaningful Christ's sufferings and substitutionary death are for me personally during times of prayer. When I pray, I often consider the consequences that my sins have brought upon the whole of creation along with those of many sinners. It is then that I feel the weight and guilt over multitudes of animals that literally eat one another to survive as a consequence of my rebellion and pride.

On a Monday morning, at the very moment when I was in thought about this, I read Romans 8:19, 23: "For the anxious longing of the creation waits eagerly for the revealing of the sons of God … For we know that the whole creation groans and suffers the pains of childbirth together until now."

I ran over a cat and heard its body crushed under the weight of my car. I had not killed a person made to reflect God's image, a person who could conceptualize the character, nature, and attributes of the eternal Creator. I had crushed "an unreasoning animal," in the words of the apostle Peter, "born as creatures of instinct to be captured and killed" (2 Peter 2:12). I had not killed a man capable of fellowshipping with the living God, but that did not keep me from being devastated by what I considered to be a horrible event in my life. I understand that I have caused—by the contribution of my sin, the callousness of my sinful heart, and the insensitivity of my reckless mouth—the suffering and death of the Son of God.

Praise God that this life is just the beginning and that the greatest joy is yet to be. All of us who trust in Jesus and not our own good works will enter into eternal life. The apostle Paul wrote the magnificent truth of Romans 8 to a church of true Christians, not those who were "Christian" in name only. The true Christian groans over his sin, and during times of repentance he does not make light of his sin but feels the full weight of how it caused the sufferings of Christ. The true Christian can make sense of the craziness of this present life, and even though he mourns over tragedy, he does so with a living hope. "For I consider that the sufferings of this present time are not worthy to be compared with the glory that is to be revealed to us" (Romans 8:18).

The first thought to enter my mind after crushing that cat was the death of the Son of God who was crushed for my transgressions (Isaiah 53:5). His was the plan to rescue me from before the foundation of the world, but it was my sins that caused His suffering and death. It is no small matter to cause God's suffering. I cannot explain why God pours out His grace only upon some, while others will experience their just judgment. What I do know is that God has uttered a decree. "Enter through the narrow gate; for the gate is wide and the way is broad that leads to destruction, and there are many who enter through it. For the gate is small and the way is narrow that leads to life, and there are few who find it" (Matthew 7:13–14).

I know that it is by grace and not my goodness that I am saved. "For by grace you have been saved through faith; and not of yourselves, it is a gift of God; not as a result of works, so that no one may boast" (Ephesians 2:8–9). The apostle Paul wrote "you *have been* saved" in past tense—when Jesus died on the cross for my sins. My salvation became experientially real to me in 1967 when I trusted Christ as the only means of eternal life. However, Jesus completed the work for my salvation two thousand years ago as He hung between heaven and hell, rejected by men and punished by God.

I am nothing but a lost sinner saved by God's grace. How often I have complained about the circumstances of my life. I have rationalized selfishness, justified bad behavior, and defended my wrongs. But when Jesus was faced with the penalty of my transgressions, innocent though He was, He opened not His mouth. "And while He was being accused by the chief priests and elders, He did not answer" (Matthew 27:12).

At the heart of all acceptable worship is the recognition that one has caused the death of the Son of God. For this reason, Jesus said to His followers, literally hours before His sacrificial death, "I am the way, and the truth, and the life; no one comes to the Father but through Me" (John 14:6). The person who is a true Christian in deed does not merely accept intellectual facts about Jesus. Neither is Jesus merely a sentimental attraction or a tradition to follow because of allegiance with family members.

To know Jesus means separation from the world, going against the tide of humanity, and a rebirth that could cost you your life—and it surely will change your philosophical perspective. The true Jesus is not one who fixes a sinful life by adding more sinful lusts and desires to it. The true Jesus is the one who eradicates condemning sins from the record of those whom the Father has chosen to receive His unmerited grace through the sacrifice of His beloved Son.

It is *that* Jesus you need to know.

Within God Is a Heart of Transferable Love

"I in them and you in me—that they may be completely one, so that the world will know that you sent me, and you have loved them just as you have loved me." (John 17:23)

"For this reason a man shall leave his father and mother and shall be joined to his wife, and the two shall become one flesh. This mystery is great; but I am speaking with reference to Christ and the church." (Ephesians 5:31–32)

A One-Flesh Relationship:
Jesus Elevates His People to a Holy Union with God

CHAPTER 8

JESUS'S DEFINING UNION: THE ULTIMATE GOAL OF GOD'S LOVE

The main theme of this book is, as the subtitle states, a character study of the Christ. A person might ask how knowing about Christ's character affects him. The purpose of this chapter is to prove that God the Father's plan for the ages is to take the things that belong to Christ and give them to those whom He saves. Furthermore, it is equally important to understand the process by which God imparts the goodness of Christ within those He restores to fellowship with Him.

When I speak about the ultimate goal of God's love, I mean the way that it impacts people, but I do not suggest that man's needs are more important than God's glory and good pleasure. The eternal God is the Supreme Person, by whom all things exist, and apart from whom nothing can continue. The ultimate goal of the Father's love is to provide a bride for His eternal Son, and the Son's love is for the Father's good pleasure. Therefore, the glory of God far exceeds all the needs of men. Man is meant to be in relationship with God; therefore, there is an ultimate goal of God's love for men. God's ultimate goal for His people will be accomplished through a one-flesh relationship between them and Christ.

The ultimate goal of God's love is for man to experience the same love that the Father has for His Son. The means through which God accomplished His goal was to identify His Son with His people through a one-flesh relationship. A saved man experiences unity with God the Father through a one-flesh relationship with His Son. As a result of unity with God and identification with His Son, a Christian man experiences the love that the Son has with His heavenly Father. Furthermore, as the Son declares the Father's name and makes His person known, the Christian then experiences intimacy with the Father through the Son's love, which results in the Father's love for the Son being placed within his heart.

In this chapter I will explain the meaning of a one-flesh relationship. Furthermore, we will examine how unity with God is obtained through identification with Christ. Finally, we will contemplate how the love that the Father has for the Son is placed within those who experience intimacy with Christ.

A One-Flesh Relationship

The greatest mystery in the entire Bible is the one-flesh relationship between a man and a woman, which represents the union between Christ and His church. "For this reason a man shall leave his father and mother and shall be joined to his wife, and the two shall become *one flesh*. This mystery is great; but I am speaking with reference to Christ and the church" (Ephesians 5:31–32, emphasis added).

A mystery, as described in the Bible, refers to a spiritual truth revealed to the people of God through Christ, which is otherwise hidden apart from Him. Mysteries are not revealed all at once but in God's time; they are first proclaimed through prophecies during Old Testament times. In the New Testament book of Hebrews, mysteries are referred to as "a shadow of things to come." However, what was once a shadow becomes a substantial truth as clear as crystal by that which God accomplished through His beloved Son.

The word *great* in Ephesians 5:32 as used in the Greek refers to "things esteemed highly for their importance." There are no spiritual truths that are plainer, and at the same time better hidden, than those in the institution of marriage. Since Adam and Eve, men and women have been bound together in holy wedlock, formed new families, and shared their lives and dreams together. God described this joining together in this way: "And the two shall become one flesh." In this one-flesh relationship where two people share one life, God has hidden and revealed His plan for eternity. That is to say, God would become one with His people in a one-flesh relationship. This one-flesh relationship between the creature and the Creator is God's plan for eternity. Paul quoted from Genesis 2:24 and added, "For this reason a man shall leave his father and mother and shall be joined to his wife *and the two shall become one flesh.* This mystery is great; but I am speaking with, reference to Christ and the church" (emphasis added).

The relationship of a man and a woman in marriage is so intertwined with the relationship God has planned with His chosen people that Paul had to say, "*But* I am speaking with reference to Christ and the church." In other words, Paul had quoted an Old Testament passage from Genesis 2 that referred to the marriage of a man and a woman, but he was referring to Christ and the church.

Question: why is a man joined to his wife? Answer: to reflect God's plan for eternity! When a man and woman experience marital life together, they also reflect the holy union between God and man. The fruit of the relationship that men have with God is to experience the fullness of God. The union of Christ and man as a way to experience God's fullness is referenced throughout the letter to the Ephesians. Ephesians 1:23 says, "The church, which is His body, the *fullness* of Him who *fills* all in all" (emphasis added). God's fullness is accomplished through the holy union He enjoys with His people, the church. In Ephesians 2:14 we are told that Christ "who is our peace has made both groups that is Jew and Gentile into one."

And for what reason? First, Paul emphasized the union of Jew and Gentile, and then he focused on God's indwelling. Verse 22 speaks of the place of God residence, "in whom you also are being built together into a *dwelling* of God in the Spirit." Repeatedly we are told that God dwells in and with His people in a one-flesh experience. In Ephesians 3:19 we are told, "Know the love of Christ that surpasses knowledge, so that you may be *filled* up to all the *fullness* of God." In Ephesians 4:15 we are taught that by "practicing the truth in love, we will in all things grow up *into* Christ." Throughout the entire letter, Paul taught about a one-flesh relationship so that the Ephesian church might understand and experience the fullness of God.

Think of it! The creature becomes united with the Creator; the mortal becomes one with the immortal; the finite shares eternity with the infinite One. The One who is infinite in every way shares all things with those who are finite in every way, and the sinner shares glory with the holy one. This mystery hidden in marriage is revealed through the church. "Of this church I was made a minister … to whom God willed to make known what is the riches of the glory of this mystery among the Gentiles, which is Christ in you, the hope of glory" (Colossians 1:25). Marriage has been chosen by God to reflect His eternal plan. As a binding institution for a lifetime, or a one-flesh relationship "till death do us part," marriage is meant to reflect God's eternal plan.

Jesus's defining union, then, is His marriage to the church, which becomes the bride of Christ or, as stated in the book of Revelation, the bride of the Lamb. "Let us rejoice and be glad and give the glory to Him, for the marriage of the Lamb has come and His bride has made herself ready" (Revelation 19:7). It is Christ who will receive the glory for this holy union; He was the self-sacrificing Lamb slain for the sins of men in the greatest act of love that the world will ever know. Furthermore, the bride made herself fit to be the bride of the Lamb when she was washed in His blood and made clean by the person and deeds of her groom. Jesus gave Himself for His bride through the sufferings He endured on her behalf (Ephesians 5:25–27). The church is the most loved bride that has been or will ever be, for the eternal God has loved her with an everlasting love and has sacrificed Himself for her.

First, by definition, a *union* is "the act of joining together to make a whole." Man is made whole, according to what God has planned him to be, when he is joined to Christ.

Second, a *union* is also defined as "the state of marriage." The book of Genesis tells us that God first created man and then took from him a rib, which He fashioned into a woman. In the union of marriage, God made from one substance two, which He then bound together to make one, out of which He made a new person. The bone of the man was fashioned into a woman, and the woman was joined to the man, which in turn produced a new person: Abel.

There is a parallel in how God accomplished salvation through the marriage of Christ with His beloved people. The human race was first created, and then from the female part of the human race God fashioned a sinless man. The sinless man was the result of combining the seed of the woman, the Son of man, with the Son of the Most High. When the Son is then joined with a believer, a new creation results, and salvation is accomplished.

Third, and finally, a *union* is "a fabric made of two or more different yarns, e.g., cotton and linen." In this definition we have pictured for us the creation that results from Christ being joined to His new people. We see the glory of Christ as He is joined to His beloved and the two in union fulfill the Father's will and create a new people. The institution of marriage as recorded in Genesis 2 foreshadows the marriage of the Lamb to the church.

The Individual New Man

It is important to understand that there is the *corporate* new man, which is different from the *individual* new man. The work that Jesus did to redeem (buy back) sinners from the bondage of sin is twofold: (1) God's kingdom is about communal living and (2) God is relational and has made man to be relational. God does not create community at the cost of the individual. A community is only as good as each individual within the society.

Paul declared to the Ephesian believers the reality of their new man in Christ as individuals within the new corporate body. Each individual person within the human race has been corrupted by sin; therefore, each person needs to be renewed through the person and work of Christ. "That, in reference to your former manner of life, you lay aside the old self, which is being corrupted in accordance with the lusts of deceit, and that you be renewed in the spirit of your mind, and put on the new self, which in the likeness of God has been created in righteousness and holiness of the truth" (Ephesians 4:22–24).

According to these verses, the lusts of deceit corrupt the old self, which results in a manner of life that corrupts the image of God, which ends in death. However, as a result of marriage with Christ, a man can be renewed in the spirit of his mind, and he can put on his new self, which is created in an accurate image of God. The experience stated in verses 22–44 is dependent upon the accomplished work of Christ at His death, which can then become a present reality through the exercise of a sinner's God-given faith. The new self has then been created. That creation took place at the moment the person received Christ, and it is then activated by faith continually. "For in it (the gospel) the righteousness of God is revealed from faith to faith; as it is written, 'But the righteous man shall live by faith.'" The basis for the new life is a work accomplished in Christ two thousand years ago. It is the work of God and not man. It is, however, received by faith.

The Corporate New Man

Just as Christ lives within the individual believer in order to make a new man, He also lives within the body corporate to make a new race, people group, and society. Paul, in the context of the following verses, makes the point that Christ has removed the dividing wall between Jew and Gentile, which was created by the law, ordinances, and covenants when God chose them as His people. The law could not save, and neither could a covenant made by sinners bent on breaking the law and the covenants. When Christ died, He put to death the law of commandments so that through Him a new man might be created, and peace would be established.

"Remember that you were at that time separate from Christ, excluded from the commonwealth of Israel, and strangers to the covenants of promise, having no hope and without God in the world ... For He Himself is our peace, who made both groups into one and broke down the barrier of the dividing wall, By abolishing in His flesh the enmity, which is the Law of commandments contained in ordinances, so that in Himself He might make the two into one new man, thus establishing peace" (Ephesians 2:12, 14–15).

The one new man spoken of in verse 15 is the community of God's people, which by virtue of their newness in Christ can be referred to as *a man*, singular. Division is not a characteristic of this new people. Of course, perfection is not obtained this side of heaven, but it will be in Christ's coming kingdom. It behooves all of God's people to set as priority this new unity within the body of Christ. The union that Christ has with His people then is both corporate and particular or for each person.

Furthermore, the holy union of marriage between the Christ and man has two defining characteristics. First, the man who is *identified* with Christ in His death also shares His glory so that he might experience unity with his brethren as Jesus does with His Father. Second, the man who comes to know the Father intimately through His Son also receives in his heart the Father's love for His Son, and Jesus dwells there.

Unity through Identification with Christ

Identification is defined as "a powerful feeling of affinity with another person or group, which sometimes involves regarding somebody as a model and adopting his or her beliefs, values, or other characteristics." In order for God to fulfill His original plan to make man in His own image, He had to ensure that the creation identified with Christ. In his identification with Christ, God takes man to a higher level of conformity to Himself. Therefore, the fallen but recovered sinner desires fully to become like his Savior in the way He thinks, wills, and feels, and he is transformed into God's image.

At the cross, Jesus took the sinner's place, thereby identifying Himself with each and every sinner for whom He died. Thus the sinner could be counted righteous in Christ's place. It is through identification that the sinner is united to Christ. This holy union is compared to the union between the Father and the Son in Jesus's high-priestly prayer as recorded in John 17. "The glory which You have given Me I have given to them, that they may be one, just as We are one; I in them and You in Me, that they may be perfected in unity, so that the world may know that You sent Me, and loved them, even as You have loved Me" (John 17:22–23).

There has always been a holy unity between the Father and the Son, and it is this unity that is created in a people whom Christ has saved by His sacrificial death. "I in them and You in Me, that they may be perfected in unity" (John 17:23). Just as the Son dwells in His people, the Father dwells in the Son, so God's people may be perfected in divine unity. To be in Christ is likened to being in a house: it's a place to take up residence and find security, rest, and a place to call your own. To be in Christ is to call Him our own and to recognize that we belong to Him.

Acting on fleshly desires and physical impulses in thought and deed prior to marriage—or with others after being married—is a sin against God's design for a holy union. God's design for the marriage of His Son does not include fleshly impulses at all, but rather intellectual and emotional unity that results in faithful choices that are always moral and loving. Sexual union between a man and a woman is a gift from God that expands the race and helps to cement the relationship as exclusive to one another. Sin distorts that sacred act and twists it into something evil, selfish, and completely at odds with God's original design. Anything other than an exclusive union with God is idolatry, which is akin to adultery. In either case, it breaks the covenant relationship and corrupts the image of the Trinitarian God.

By creating a holy union between the eternal Son and a fallen humanity, God created a new man who is able to experience divine love and thereby bring divine unity to a new race of redeemed men. "Holy Father, keep them in Your name, the name which You have given Me, that they may be one even as We are" (John 17:11). The cruelty and divisiveness of the world is born out of the self-centeredness of the human heart, which is the fruit of sinful pride. Each man goes his own way without concern for others; he looks out for himself and his own to the exclusion of others. There is an unholy selfishness in the world to mass proportions, and even within individual families. God set out to undo all the selfishness and self-centeredness of men by sending Christ into the world. He lived completely unselfishly, for the Father's will and for His glory and pleasure. When Christ died, He took the evil of men into the grave; and when He rose from the dead, they rose from the dead by identification with Him. His devotion to the Father's will becomes their devotion to the Father's will. Devotion to the Father's will among the brethren translates into unity with one another. By identifying with sinful men, Jesus made it possible for sinful men to love one another.

> By identifying with sinful men, Jesus made it possible for sinful men to love one another.

When Jesus identified with sinful men, He brought to fruition a holy union between God and His people. It is in that union that the last part of verse 11 is fulfilled: "that they may be one even as We are." The name by which God keeps his people is *Lord*! "At the name of Jesus every knee will bow, of those who are in heaven and on earth and under the earth, and that every tongue will confess that Jesus Christ is Lord, to the glory of God the Father" (Philippians 2:10–11).

When all men bow to the same Lord and obey all the same decrees, commands, and desires, they are one. Only when we identify with Jesus in His death do we obey Him in His life. In order for all of God's people to be one, they must all obey the same Lord, which is why it is so important to study and obey His Word. Agreement is important, because it makes us one with the one with whom we agree. The words of Amos 3:3 are applicable at this point. "Do two walk together, unless they have agreed to meet?" Agreement is at the very heart of unity. To agree to meet at the altar of Jesus's lordship is the essence of divine unity.

The Father Loves the Church as He Loves His Son

Within God is a heart of transferrable love as stated in John 17:23: "I in them and you in me—that they may be completely one, so that the world will know that you sent me, and you have loved them just as you have loved me." In order for God to love a man to the extent that He loves His Son, He has to unite the man to His Son so that when He sees the man He sees His Son. The sacrifice of the Son took place so that man could be loved with the same love with which the Father loves the Son.

The Father loves the Son, knowing full well that He is worthy of His love. God could not love created man the way He loves His infinitely holy and perfect Son who alone is worthy of the Father's love. It would be impossible for man to be seen as equal with the Son, because the Son is intrinsically and infinitely holy, and man is merely a created being. Only when the Son is united with a man—to such an extent that when the Father sees the man He sees His Son—could the Father love the man as His Son.

Herein lies salvation's plan: the Father desired a bride for His Son in order to obtain one that was worthy of His Son, and He would have to unite His Son to her in a holy and costly union. In Paul's letter to the

Romans, we are told in no uncertain terms that the salvation of man cost the Father His own Son. "He who did not spare His own Son, but delivered Him over for us all, how will He not also with Him freely give us all things?" (Romans 8:32) The love with which the Father loves the Son He bestowed on those who belong to the Son. Now that is unconditional love! In eternity the saved bride will receive all things that the Son possesses, and in our present context, that includes the love He receives from the Father.

Any child of God who is feeling overwhelmed by the trials of life merely needs to dwell on the love of God as revealed in the truth that his or her identity is found in Christ the Son, and to understand that throughout eternity God will see him or her just as He sees His Son. Furthermore, this relationship is not merely a judicial one but one in experience, so God's will, desires, mind, and emotions will be reproduced in His believing children.

Whether the trial you face is physical, financial, sinful, worldly, demonic, mental, or emotional, an eternal perspective is needed. Paul gave the Christian such a perspective when He wrote, "For I consider that the sufferings of this present time are not worthy to be compared with the glory that is to be revealed to us." This glory is the presence of the Son of God, which will become in him a well of water springing up to eternal life.

On the one side of salvation, man is *identified* with Christ in His death, shares His glory, and experiences the same unity with his brethren that Jesus does with His Father. On the second side of salvation, man comes to know the Father intimately through His Son and receives in his heart the Father's love for His Son, where Jesus also dwells.

Love through Intimacy with Christ

"O righteous Father, although the world has not known You, yet I have known You; and these have known that You sent Me; and I have made Your name known to them, and will make it known, so that the love with which You loved Me may be in them, and I in them" (John 17:25–26).

Technically, *intimacy* means "a detailed knowledge resulting from a close or long association or study." It is God's desire to have sweet and intimate communion with individual men, and in so doing to make

Himself known. Apart from direct revelation from God about Himself, there is no way that a man can obtain such knowledge. "For God, who said, 'Light shall shine out of darkness,' is the One who has shone in our hearts to give the Light of the knowledge of the glory of God in the face of Christ" (1 Corinthians 4:6). Apart from the light of God shining into a man's heart, he remains in darkness; but when God shines, the knowledge of His glory is revealed through Christ.

Looking at Christ face to face and eye to eye is an expression depicting the ability to look inside the heart and soul of God. The knowledge that Christ imparts in His people is not merely for the sake of imparting knowledge, but it is so that the love of Christ might dispel all the wickedness in the human heart and replace it with God's goodness. The knowledge of God is always meant to end in worship. The goodness of God is expressed in the letter to the Galatians as the fruit of the spirit, which is joy, peace, patience, kindness, goodness, faithfulness, gentleness, and self-control. Jesus prayed to the Father and declared that He had made known to His disciples the Father's name so that the love of the Father might be in them. "I have made Your name known to them, and will make it known, so that the love with which You loved Me may be in them, and I in them" (John 17:26). Christ Himself is imparted to the people of the Father's choosing, and thereby the love that emanates from His heart also emanates from theirs. Therefore, the Father goes beyond viewing the bride with the same love that He has for His Son to imparting the Son in the bride, and thereby imparting the Son's love in them.

Furthermore, Jesus said, "I have made Your name known to them ... so that the love with which You loved Me may be in them." Jesus said that His love is imparted through making the Father's name known. At this point we may question the validity of William Shakespeare's statement, "What is in a name?" In the Greek language the word *name* carries the meaning of everything that the name stands for or depicts. By definition a name depicts "everything which the name covers, everything the thought or feeling of which is aroused in the mind by mentioning, hearing, remembering, the name, i.e., for one's rank, authority, interests, pleasure, command, excellences, deeds, etc."

When Paul wrote to the Philippian believers, he told them how unselfish Christ was when He laid aside His infinite divine attributes and put on the finiteness of humanity. He then exhorted them to put on Jesus's attitude (Philippians 2:5–8). Paul then went on to say, "Work out your salvation with fear and trembling." Paul immediately told us how the Christian can work out his salvation by a holy union with God who is at work within him. "For it is God who is at work in you, both to will and to work for His good pleasure" (Philippians 2:3).

The Christian is anything but alone, but he has been brought into intimate fellowship with the living God, who Himself is humble and willing to lay aside His noncommunicative attributes (omniscience, omnipotence, etc.) in order to rescue sinners from the destructive force of internal sin. Christ emptied Himself, and as a man He took the form of a slave and became obedient to death so that sinful men could be set free from the bondage of slavery.

God is loving above all created beings. Nonetheless, the Christian should work out his salvation with fear and trembling, because God is within Him in a holy union where two have become *one* flesh.

When Paul wrote to the Corinthian believers, he put it this way:

> Do you not know that your bodies are members of Christ? Shall I then take away the members of Christ and make them members of a prostitute? May it never be! Or do you not know that the one who joins himself to a prostitute is one body with her? For He says, "The two shall become one flesh." But the one who joins himself to the Lord is one spirit with Him. Flee immorality. Every other sin that a man commits is outside the body, but the immoral man sins against his own body. Or do you not know that your body is a temple of the Holy Spirit who is in you, whom you have from God, and that you are not your own? For you have been bought with a price: therefore glorify God in your body. (1 Corinthians 6:15–20)

Verse 17 is a key verse in this section, because in it Paul declared the union of God with His people as a marital union: "The two shall become one flesh." Then he went beyond an earthly marriage to say that God and a man are one in spirit: "But the one who joins himself to the

Lord is one spirit with Him." Again the scripture makes it perfectly clear that the relationship between God and the people He redeems is a *one-flesh* relationship, just as in the relationship of marriage and penetrating even deeper. The union of God with men is one of shared desires, goals, character traits, love, devotion, perspective, etc. God takes up residence in a man's being as man dwells within Him through His Holy Spirit.

Think about the one who takes up residence within the human soul. Paul refers to our Lord this way: "He who is the blessed and only Sovereign, the King of kings and Lord of lords, who alone possesses immortality and *dwells in unapproachable light*, whom *no man has seen or can see*. To Him be honor and eternal dominion! Amen" (1 Timothy 6:15–16, emphasis added). It is in this state that men need to fear and tremble—not because God does not love them, but because He who is unapproachable is present within them.

The Christian is not perfect, even though he is saved and indwelled by God the Holy Spirit. For this reason he must live near the cross of Christ's sufferings and love Him all his days. "This is eternal life, that they may know You, the only true God, and Jesus Christ whom You have sent" (John 17:3). To know God in this way is to know Him personally—not just to know facts about Him, but to have personal knowledge of Him, to be friends and not hostile to Him—which is only made possible through the sufferings of Christ.

It is vitally important to understand that God has planned to fulfill His own will through jars of clay, transformed sinners, men formed from the dust of the ground—in short, through the creature, and a fallen sinner at that. How then can God bring about his perfect, holy, and transcendent will through such vessels? In John 17:23 we read that the love the Father has for the Son is given to sinful men through the Son. "I in them and you in me—that they may be completely one, so that the world will know that you sent me, and you have loved them just as you have loved me." Sinful men receive the love that is meant for the Son of God.

In John 17:26 the same love that is bestowed upon sinful men returns again to the God who bestowed it. "I have made Your name known to them, and will make it known, so that the love with which You loved Me may be in them, and I in them." In this verse we see that the love of God placed within a man returns again to the God who imparted it. A man must first receive love from God before he will be able to return it. We are merely empty conduits through which the Creator works His divine will. The Christian is set free to love, enabled to love, and will be held accountable for love.

However, at the judgment God will get all the glory—and it is right that He does so. The sentiments of this thought were voiced by the great theologian Augustine of Hippo when he prayed to God, "Grant what you command and command what you desire." The apostle John said it this way: "We love because he first loved us" (1 John 4:19).

> Near, so near am I to God,
> Nearer I cannot be;
> For in the Person of His Son,
> I'm just as near as He.

> Dear, so dear am I to God,
> Dearer I cannot be;
> The love wherewith He loved His Son,
> Such is His love for me.

In America in the twentieth century, there has a been a deterioration of the holiday we call Thanksgiving. Once upon a time it was festive, taking center stage as people entered into the Christmas spirit. But no more. Thanksgiving has been replaced by a sense of entitlement. Gratitude toward God has been replaced by a belief that all things come into being by accident, by chance. Thanksgiving is a lost sentiment among people who think they deserve everything, always desire to have more, and are jealous for what they do not possess. Such characteristics should never be present in the sinner who has been saved by God's grace.

Instead a keen sense of gratitude should carry the day. Christians should spend much time on their faces before God, in humble submission to the words of scripture as the knowledge of salvation washes over their conscience. The presence of the living God within the believer is too great to contemplate, really. It should bring a sense of worship and awe to the Christian who stands in the place of Jesus's disciples so long ago when they saw Him calm the wind and the sea. The Christian should be heard saying, as they did, "What kind of a man is this, that even the winds and the sea obey Him?" (Matthew 8:27).

When the Christian contemplates the holy union he has with the living and eternal God, he should frequently find himself flat on his face, uttering the words of Peter: "Depart from me Lord, for I am a sinful man" (Luke 5:8). Then he should pick himself up from the ground as he remembers that the sufferings of Christ, which brought about his reconciliation with God, and walk in obedience, knowing that God is with him. If the true Christian stays on his face and does not work for the Lord, he denies his forgiveness and becomes weak in faith. If he does not return again to God in repentance, humility, and awe, he will arise again in pride and become weak in faith. The Christian should live in faith that is first humble and then obedient. The unrepentant sinner can do none of the above. His heart can only be insincere and full of self-deception.

You need to know Jesus, because apart from Him you will never know the holy union that alone can make you complete. No spouse on the face of the earth can complete you as Jesus can. Jesus alone is your reason for being. He is the love you have been waiting for and the culmination of every good and holy dream.

Within God Is a Heart of Everlasting Love

"This hope we have as an anchor of the soul, a hope both sure and steadfast and one which enters within the veil, where Jesus has entered as a forerunner for us, having become a high priest forever according to the order of Melchizedek." (Hebrews 6:19–20)

"For this Melchizedek ... having neither beginning of days nor end of life, but made like the Son of God, he remains a priest perpetually." (Hebrews 7:2–3)

"Who has become such not on the basis of a law of physical requirement, but according to the power of an indestructible life." (Hebrews 7:16)

"For it is attested of Him, 'You are a priest forever.'" (Hebrews 7:17)

"The Lord has sworn and will not change His mind. 'You are a priest forever.'" (Hebrews 7:21; Psalms 110:4)

"But Jesus, on the other hand, because He continues forever, holds His priesthood permanently." (Hebrews 7:24)

"Therefore He is able also to save forever those who draw near to God through Him, since He always lives to make intercession for them." (Hebrews 7:25)

"For the Law appoints men as high priests who are weak, but the word of the oath, which came after the Law, appoints a Son, made perfect forever." (Hebrews 7:28)

Jesus Lives Forever as a Man to Intercede for His People

CHAPTER 9

Jesus's Eternal Priesthood: The Duration of God's Love

Why is there a chapter about Jesus's eternal priesthood?

The first question that must be answered in order to understand the meaning behind anything written is this: *why* was it written? Intent is the necessary component when assessing the meaning. John gives us the answer in his first letter: "These things I have written to you who believe in the name of the Son of God, so that you may know that you have eternal life" (John 5:13). There is no greater peace, joy, and contentment than that which proceeds from assurance of eternal life. What does it matter that there is suffering during the brief time we have in this life, if a person is assured that there is only happiness for him or her throughout eternity?

Assurance of salvation for the Christian is based upon the character of Jesus Christ. John wrote to those who already *believed in the name of the Son of God,* and what he wanted them to understand was the meaning of that name. The names of God identify His attributes. They describe who and what He is in His divine person. It is the character of God the Father working through the person of His Son in the believer that assures the believer of sinless perfection throughout eternity.

I have heard it said that because the Christian receives a resurrected body he or she will never again sin—as if there were something special about the body. However, Jesus lived a perfect and sinless life in a body just like the ones we are living in now. It is unreasonable to assume that it is the body that will make the difference between sinning and not sinning.

During the writing of this chapter I asked my wife, "Why will the

Christian no longer sin in eternity?" She replied, "Because Jesus died so that we would no longer sin." Her answer was perfectly correct because her answer was Jesus. Specifically, it is Jesus's person and work—for and in the believer—that transforms him into sinless perfection in eternity. How, then, can we have the full assurance of hope right here and now?

Assurance of Hope

Proverbs 13:12 says, "Hope deferred makes the heart sick, but desire fulfilled is a tree of life." Any person who has lived life for any amount of time can agree that the psalmist knew exactly what he was talking about when he spoke about hope. A person with hope desires some good thing to take place. Surely everyone knows the feeling of exhilaration when his or her hope is fulfilled. Likewise, hope deferred can be quite devastating to the soul.

I once read that man can live thirty days without food, three days without water, three minutes without air, but only about three seconds without hope. I believe the principle behind that statement is true. A man without hope is a man with no reason to live. How do I know? Just take purpose out of a person's heart and watch what happens to his or her demeanor. Some purposes that people have are good and healthy, and some are evil and destructive, but all people have purpose for living.

There is one major difference between worldly hope and divine hope: worldly hope has no certain guarantee that it will ever come to pass. Divine hope has the certainty of God, who has all the power necessary to bring a thing to pass, and the strength of character to never break His promise. The great explorer Juan Ponce de León is well known for seeking after the Fountain of Youth, but after becoming the first governor of Puerto Rico, he died. The hope of eternal life can only be found by looking to Jesus.

The highest purpose for living is to glorify God our Creator and to thank Him for salvation. The main subject matter of this chapter is the hope of eternal life that is given to all those who lay hold of God's promises. The Christian life may be likened unto a man who has had great financial resources placed in a bank on his behalf. The resources belong to him. He can take a withdrawal at anytime without any questions being asked. He must, however, make a withdrawal in order to benefit from the resources.

One of the resources placed in the bank on the Christian's behalf is divinely inspired hope. We are told in Hebrews 6:17–18 that in order for God to show the heirs of the promise the unchangeableness of His purpose, He intervened by making an oath. The reason for the oath is to encourage those who take refuge in God's promises because they know that God is faithful. He has never broken His word, and He never will. The power behind the oath God made is the strength of His integrity.

No one should ever underestimate the importance and necessity of hope, because hope is the thing out of which perseverance is made. Only those who finish the race receive the prize. Because hope is so important, God made sure that it is always available. There is great assurance in the way God communicates to His people the hope set before them.

God intervened with an oath and thereby gave a twofold assurance of hope. First, God cannot lie, which means that what He has said is trustworthy. Second, He never changes, which means that He will never change His mind. "Jesus Christ the same yesterday, and today, and forever" (Hebrews 13:8). "Every good gift and every perfect gift is from above, coming down from the Father of lights with whom there is no variation or shadow due to change" (James 1:7). God is perfect and complete. Therefore, He never changes, which means that every characteristic of God remains the same eternally. God took a vow that Jesus Christ is a priest forever. Therefore, because God promised—and He does not lie or change His mind—we can be doubly assured that His promise is eternally secure.

Hebrews 7 gives seven reasons for a full assurance of hope.

Seven Reasons for a Full Assurance of Hope

The author of Hebrews gave us seven reasons for assurance from the High Priestly ministry of Christ that His priesthood will continue forever. The reader can be assured that His salvation is an eternal one laced with eternal rewards. Then he will not lose hope or grow weary in doing what is right. The seven reasons given would mean nothing if not for the underlying character of Christ upon which they are all built. Let the reader then consider these seven reasons for a full assurance of hope, set forth for those who take refuge in the promises of God.

Reason 1: Jesus Is an Eternal Priest

Hebrews 7 begins with an account of the person called Melchizedek, who appears in Genesis 14. "Without father, without mother, without genealogy, he has neither beginning of days nor end of life but is like the son of God, and he remains a priest for all time" (Hebrews 7:3). The author of Hebrews refers to Melchizedek as a picture of a new priesthood, a priest who was not part of the first priesthood under Law of Moses. In Genesis 14:8 Melchizedek was referred to as a priest of the Most High God, so the picture of a new priesthood is not without sufficient warrant. Psalms 110 also makes reference to Melchizedek, which, when combined with Hebrews, makes a three-strand "cord," which according to the scriptures is not easily broken.

The prominent thought in this verse, which is also true of the entire chapter, is the longevity with which Jesus holds His office of High Priest. Christ as Melchizedek is without beginning of days or end of life, which means He can remain a priest forever. It is this thought that is meant to give the Christian a full assurance of hope. Jesus is never going to change His mind, and God is never going to go back on His promise. Like the picture given as far back as Genesis, Christ will intercede forever.

The primary work of a high priest is one of intercession. He is a moderator or mediator between two parties. Jesus offered Himself as a sacrifice and thereby totally eradicated the penalty of sin before God. No more intercession is necessary to satisfy God's justice, because it was dealt with perfectly on the cross to which Jesus was nailed. The author confirms this truth in chapters 9 and 10 so that his hearers will not be confused —after he first elaborates that Jesus has become the mediator of a new covenant in chapters 7 and 8.

The intercession referred to in Hebrews 7 is one of standing between God and men on a continuing basis once the relationship has been restored. The new covenant is primarily about a new heart, which we will look at in more detail as we consider the second reason for a full assurance of hope.

Reason 2: Jesus Is an Indestructible Priest

"Who has become such not on the basis of a law of physical requirement, but according to the power of an indestructible life" (Hebrews 7:16).

Under the law as it was delivered to Moses, a ceremonial system was established by which the people could have their sins removed once a year by the sacrificial offering of an animal. The high priest entered once every year past the veil that separated God from the privileged Levites who ministered before the Lord year round. The offerings were animals, and the high priest was chosen from among the tribe of Levi, his term lasting until his death. Therefore, there was a continual procession of high priests as each died in succession. The animal sacrifice was only good for one year, as it was only a picture of the perfect and sufficient sacrifice yet to come.

Under the New Covenant, the High Priest described in Hebrews 7 is one "who has become such not on the basis of a law of physical requirement, but according to the power of an indestructible life" (Hebrews 7:16). The first priesthood consisted of the descendants of Aaron, and the covenant required men to do all that was written in the law (Deuteronomy 30:15–17). The Old Covenant was replaced by a new one in which the terms were completely different.

The author of Hebrews 7 quoted the New Covenant as declared by the prophet Jeremiah: "For this is the covenant that I will make with the house of Israel after those days, says the Lord: I will put My laws into their minds, and I will write them on their hearts. And I will be their God, and they shall be My people" (Jeremiah 31:31–34).

The covenant was changed from a demand placed upon men to obey God, to an act of God to place His own law in the minds and hearts of its recipients. It is this placing of the law within the mind and heart of the believer that then becomes the ministry of the High Priest for all eternity. One day the saints will be perfect and without any sin, but until that day, Jesus will intercede on behalf of believers and rescue them out of their sins.

We catch a glimpse of Jesus's intercession for Peter from His words: "Simon, Simon, behold, Satan has demanded permission to sift you like wheat; but I have prayed for you, that your faith may not fail" (Luke 22:31–32). Peter's faith faltered temporarily, but because of Jesus's intercession, his faith was restored. Even though the believer may sin in this present life, he has an advocate with the Father: Jesus Christ, the righteous. In Him man's sins are forgiven, the power of sin is broken, and his relationship is renewed on the basis of Jesus's atoning sacrifice.

However, a day is coming when the believer will be in a state of sinless perfection. He will be joined to Christ, the Son of God, in an unbreakable union that will usher forth in unparalleled godliness. Christ will forever represent God, who dwells in unapproachable light, because man apart from Christ could never be joined in marriage to God. Christ as High Priest will continually intercede between God and men by the work of the Holy Spirit. He will send forth the very character of God into the hearts of His people, place His laws into their minds, and reflect His own glory through man, who is continually being made into Christ's holy image. As man could never drink in the oceans of the world in one sitting, so man can never fully acquire all the fullness of God. But throughout eternity he will continually drink in the presence of God through Christ by the Holy Spirit who dwells within him.

The assurance of our hope in this perfected state of communion with God is placed squarely upon the shoulders of Jesus Christ, who is said to be a High Priest according to the power of an indestructible life. In the Greek, *akatálutos* (indestructible) means "that which cannot be caused to cease, cannot be brought to an end, cannot be caused to finish, and thus is indestructible and indissoluble." All that has been said about Jesus's high-priestly ministry will never come to an end, because He is indestructible. The full assurance of hope is built upon the indissoluble person and character of the Son of God.

The third reason for a full assurance of hope is built upon the declaration made by God through His servant David.

Reason 3: Jesus Is Declared to Be a Priest Forever

"For it is attested of Him, 'You are a Priest forever according to the order of Melchizedek'" (Psalms 110:4).

In Hebrews 6 and 7, the author returns to Psalms 110:4 repeatedly in order to clarify the psalmist's use of the historical person of Melchizedek. In so doing, he compounds the evidence for the divine decree concerning Jesus's high-priestly ministry found in Genesis 14 and Psalms 110. The focal point of Hebrews 7:17 is the testimony of God concerning the Messiah's role as High Priest. The psalm was written by David, and it begins with the very famous words: "The Lord says to my Lord: 'Sit at My right hand until I make Your enemies a footstool for Your feet'" (Psalms 110:1).

It is this verse that Jesus used to bring down the house, so to speak, upon the Pharisees' heads when He asked these questions: "How is it that they say the Christ is David's son? For David himself says in the book of Psalms, 'The Lord said to my Lord, "Sit at my right hand, until I make your enemies a footstool for your feet."' Therefore David calls Him 'Lord,' and how is He his son?" (Luke 20:41–44).

A father never calls his son *Lord*; it just is not done. But in this psalm David wrote, "The Lord [the name of God as Master of the universe] said to my Lord [the same name is used, which was understood to be the coming Messiah]." Jesus used this scripture to undeniably identify the Messiah, who was clearly to be David's son—as well as David's Lord, Master/God, and Messiah.

It is in this setting that the author of Hebrews made clear the testimony of God concerning the Messiah's high-priestly ministry. "For it is attested of Him, 'You are a Priest forever according to the order of Melchizedek'" (Hebrews 7:17). The author of Hebrews was telling us is that God testified in Psalms 110:4 that Messiah was a priest *forever*. The author said that the Messiah's high-priestly ministry was not according to the Levitical requirement (verse 16) but that His life was indestructible. Then he went on to say that God testified that Messiah was a priest *forever*. Herein lies the full assurance of hope that the writer wanted us to understand and have, which is built upon the compounded proof of promises stated in Genesis 14 and Psalms 110, and explained in Hebrews 7.

The Lord made a phenomenal decree as prophesied by David and recorded in the scriptures: "*You are* a priest forever." God declared Messiah, the Son of God, to be a priest through His use of the words "you are." God, unlike man, makes decrees that always come to pass. His grace may interrupt His judgment, which is His right, but in that case His judgment falls upon His Son. The Lord finished off His decree with the incomprehensible words of eternal servitude: "You are a priest *forever.*"

Reason 4: Jesus Is a Priest by Divine Oath

"The Lord has sworn and will not change His mind, 'You are a priest forever'" (Hebrews 7:21).

When a man takes an oath, it may come to pass or it may not, for there are always many variables to be considered—which are not in play when it comes to God. A man cannot guarantee anything in this life, which is why James tells us that it is arrogance to say we will do this or that, but that we should rather say we will do this or that if the Lord wills that we live. Truthfully, we cannot guarantee that we will live from one moment to the next, no matter how old or young we are. God, however, can guarantee everything He decides to do with complete assurance by virtue of the fact that He is God and all power is in His hands. He is infinite and complete in every way.

Verse 21 declares to us that "the Lord" (*Adonai* in Hebrew) or the Master, sovereign ruler of all His creation, has taken an oath. And to whom did the Lord swear? God used the second person "you" when He said, "You are a priest forever." God the Father was speaking to God the Son when making an oath, so the reader can understand that God promised to *Himself* that He would intercede for His people forever. This is no small matter. When God swears to anyone, it is serious, but when God sears *to Himself*, He is swearing to the one person in the universe who really matters. No one can exist without God, and only an egotistical maniac would think himself to be as great as God. When God swore, He swore to the greatest person there is: Himself.

The author emphasized this same truth in the preceding chapter. "For when God made the promise to Abraham, since He could swear by no one greater, He swore by Himself" (Hebrews 6:13).

God took an oath that Messiah would be a priest forever, and then He compounded His oath by saying He would not change His mind. In order for the reader to fully grasp the assurance set before him, he must understand who it is that will not change His mind. "The Lord" is another name of God, and there is nothing and no one that can override God, and God by virtue of His integrity will not change His mind. He does not break His promises, because He is faithful to what He has said. This is a great hope and encouragement for the person who has come to know and understand who and what God is.

Therefore, the Lord will not change His mind, and Jesus Christ is a high priest *forever.*

Reason 5: Jesus Is a Priest Continually

"The former priests, on the one hand, existed in greater numbers because they were prevented by death from continuing, but Jesus, on the other hand, because He continues forever, holds His priesthood permanently" (Hebrews 7:23–24).

In Hebrews 7:24 the author used the word *permanently,* which in the Greek means literally "not pass away." It means more than incidental permanence or something that simply will not be changed. It means unchangeable, unalterable, and inviolable. It is something that *cannot* be changed. Jesus holds His priesthood permanently because He cannot be changed. I want my reader to understand that the writer of the letter to the Hebrews compounds the truth of Jesus's eternal priesthood seven times in chapter 7, and by these undeniable truths, the Christian can have an unchanging hope.

He was building a house of stones where each stone is as strong as the one upon which it is placed. Each stone of chapter 7 points to the unchangeable character of God in Jesus Christ. Jesus's priesthood is permanent, and the author continued to build a case for that permanence, like a great musical piece building to a great crescendo. The crescendo of this chapter is coming very soon, and I want my readers to be ready for it, to see it coming a little way off. And when it appears, I want him to glory in the magnificence of God in Christ.

Reason 6: Jesus Always Lives to Make Intercession

"Therefore He is able also to save forever those who draw near to God through Him, since He always lives to make intercession for them" (Hebrews 7:25).

Verse 25 can be a very confusing verse and one that does not fit well into the idea that Jesus died once for all—and that in doing so He removed the sins of His people forever. The sins of Jesus's people are never to be remembered (Hebrews 8:12; Jeremiah 31:34) but are cast into the depth of the sea (Micah 7:19). We previously discussed, under the third reason, that Jesus intercedes forever—not in forgiving sins but in uniting God and men. The union between God and men is such that the God who dwells in unapproachable light could never fellowship to the degree that He will with the church apart from the ongoing intercessory work of Christ.

"Who alone possesses immortality and dwells in unapproachable light, whom no man has seen or can see. To Him be honor and eternal dominion! Amen" (1 Timothy 6:16).

"Then Moses said, 'I pray You, show me Your glory!' And He said, 'I Myself will make all My goodness pass before you, and will proclaim the name of the Lord before you; and I will be gracious to whom I will be gracious, and will show compassion on whom I will show compassion.' But He said, 'You cannot see My face, for no man can see Me and live!'" (Exodus 33:18–20).

The work that Christ has undertaken on the sinner's behalf is beyond magnanimity and human comprehension. God's holiness is beyond anything that a created being can conceive. The being of God is like the sun in all its glory. From a distance it warms the earth and gives light and life to all that live upon it. However, whoever draws too close to its radiant glory will surely be consumed. It is not because God lacks love that a creature would be incinerated but because of the mere greatness of His consuming glory. We are so blinded by pride because of indwelling sin that we are unable to appreciate the supreme transcendency and holiness of the eternal God. Regardless of what our inclinations might tell us, the Bible makes it quite clear that God is unapproachable.

"And to the eyes of the sons of Israel the appearance of the glory of the LORD was like a consuming fire on the mountain top" (Exodus 24:17).

"And the LORD will cause His voice of authority to be heard, and the descending of His arm to be seen in fierce anger, and in the flame of a consuming fire in cloudburst, downpour and hailstones" (Exodus 30:30).

"Therefore, since we receive a kingdom which cannot be shaken, let us show gratitude, by which we may offer to God an acceptable service with reverence and awe; for our God is a consuming fire" (Hebrews 12:28–29).

"So watch yourselves, that you do not forget the covenant of the

LORD your God which He made with you, and make for yourselves a graven image in the form of anything against which the LORD your God has commanded you. For the LORD your God is a consuming fire, a jealous God" (Deuteronomy 4:23–24).

The undeniable truth that God is a consuming fire has been undermined during the past century due to saturation with the *love of God* among average churchgoers to the exclusion of *God's consuming presence*. However, when a person accepts the true reality of God's fiery holiness, he can then appreciate the extent of God's love. To fully grasp the love of God, a person must understand the extent of Christ's sacrifice.

Jesus became a man, and by so doing He limited Himself in time and space. God is infinite in space and is not controlled by time, and at the same time He became a man. It can't be explained, but it is true. When Jesus limited Himself by becoming a man, He did so for more than three hours, three days, thirty years, or even three thousand years. He did so for all eternity. No man understands what it means to be infinite, and therefore no one knows how much Christ sacrificed. To appreciate the love of God, all one need do is focus on His humble sacrifice in becoming a man forever.

In the twentieth century a great confusion arose about the terms of salvation. Some teach that a man can receive Jesus and then live like the devil all his life and still get into heaven. Others believe in the biblical doctrine of sanctification, which means that those whom the Lord saves He also transforms. The man who is justified by Christ alone and by faith alone receives heaven as a free gift, without the works of the law and completely by grace. Going into salvation, there are no works, no transformation of character, and no merit on the part of man; coming out of salvation, the Holy Spirit works to impart holiness and right choices so that men are no longer what they once were. Those who belong to God and are saved by His grace are not perfect, but they are changed, regenerate, and transformed into new and better people.

The believer is not only one who has had the penalty of his sins removed so he can stand before God as justified, but he is also one who has had his heart altered to have a true and sincere love for God. Because the believer's heart has been changed, even though it is not perfect, he can come before God through the blood of Christ and the intercessory work of the Holy Spirit (Romans 8:26–27) and be acceptable in God's sight. Therefore, the words of the psalmist are accurate: "Who may ascend into the hill of the LORD? And who may stand in His holy place? He who has clean hands and a pure heart, who has not lifted up his soul to falsehood and has not sworn deceitfully" (Psalms 24:3–4).

These words do not suggest justification alone but the sanctification that accompanies it. Therefore, the psalmist continued: "This is the generation of those who seek Him, who seek Your face—even Jacob. Selah" (Psalms 24:6). This work of renewal in the heart of the believer is not simply what takes place at the last trump when the Lord returns and His people are changed in the blink of an eye. It is an ongoing work that will continue throughout all eternity. Hence, He always lives to make intercession for His own.

William Barclay wrote, "When the writer to the Hebrews says that Jesus remains forever, there is wrapped up in that phrase the amazing thought that Jesus is forever at the service of men. In eternity as he was in time Jesus exists to be of service to mankind. That is why he is the complete Savior. On earth he served men and gave his life for them; in Heaven he still exists to make intercession for them. He is the priest forever, the one who is forever opening the door to the friendship of God and is forever the great servant of mankind."

As intercessor, Jesus prays for His beloved. He intercedes for them and labors on their behalf. It could be true that Jesus merely appears in heaven as a token of the sacrifice He offered upon the cross. However, that token of what was accomplished falls far short of the true nature of Jesus's intercession and the great crescendo to which the author of Hebrews orchestrates his chapter. In truth, Jesus sustains the souls of those He saves, and He will do so throughout eternity. Just as God sustains the material universe, in the same way He will forever sustain the spiritual nature of His beloved through the eternal sacrifice of His Son. The entire material universe is dependent upon God for its existence from microsecond to microsecond. Therefore, can the spiritual well-being of His people be less dependent upon His loving hand?

The words "I will never leave you or forsake you" take on fuller, deeper, and richer meaning as we consider the eternal nature of Jesus's eternal priesthood. It is an infinite sacrifice for God to descend from His infinite glory to become a man, and it is an equally infinite sacrifice to do so eternally. We minimize and give far less glory to Jesus if we do not consider that His sacrifice in becoming a man is an eternal one. *This is the place where we should get on our face and weep.*

The seventh reason for a full assurance of hope is yet another display of God's unending humility.

Reason 7: Jesus Christ Is a Son Made Perfect Forever

"For it was fitting for us to have such a high priest, holy, innocent, undefiled, separated from sinners and exalted above the heavens; who does not need daily, like those high priests, to offer up sacrifices, first for His own sins and then for the sins of the people, because this He did once for all when He offered up Himself. For the Law appoints men as high priests who are weak, but the word of the oath, which came after the Law, appoints a Son, made perfect forever" (Hebrews 7:26–28).

It is a little difficult for us to wrap our minds around the idea that the infinite and perfect God would have to be made into anything, and yet that is exactly what we are told. God not only lived as one of His created beings, but in the course of time He was made perfect—as if to say that He was not already perfect. In truth, God is perfect in His eternal state. However, when He entered into time and went from creating men to being one, it became necessary to learn through experience as men do. This is humility in the absolute and perfect sense of the term. This is the Jesus we all need to know.

As men, we learn best through suffering. We never appreciate what we have until we lose it, says an age-old and very true saying. The Christian is instructed to count it all joy when he encounters trials, because the testing of his faith produces patience (James 1:1, 3). In the same way that all men learn through experience and learn best through difficult experiences, the Lord Jesus Christ in His flesh became perfect through suffering. "For since He Himself was tempted in that which He has suffered, He is able to come to the aid of those who are tempted" (Hebrews 2:18).

Jesus did not endure the sufferings of the cross for kicks on a Friday afternoon. His purposes were far-reaching (forever), solemn, dignified, and befitting of the one true God. In His sacrifice He tied together the salvation that all men need and the intercession that they will forever enjoy. As God, Jesus understands all things perfectly, but as a man, Jesus learned to intercede with perfect empathy. I love the story in Joni Erickson's book about the time she was in tears in her hospital bed, and her friend told her that Jesus understood. She replied with a question: how can Jesus understand how it feels to be a quadriplegic? Her friend replied, "For six hours Jesus was nailed to a cross and could not move His arms or His legs. There is no suffering that Jesus does not understand."

Some will ask if Jesus ever lost a limb. Jesus lost the love of the Father. Which do you think is worse: losing a physical limb or the infinite love of God? As God, Jesus had experienced the eternal and unending love of an infinite God. At the cross He experienced that love for the hate of a vengeful and just God as He unleashed His righteous fury for man's sins upon Him. Now that is loss. There is no suffering that man has experienced in the history of the world that Jesus does not know infinitely more, because Jesus experienced everything as both man and God.

Jesus experienced rejection from His close friend Judas, the religious leaders who should have embraced the long-awaited Messiah, and all the people—many of whom He healed from various diseases—and He experienced it as God their Creator and humble Messiah. Jesus experienced poverty, captivity under Roman rule, the heat of the day, and the cold of the night. He knows what it means to be hungry, thirsty, tired, falsely accused, beaten, and crucified. He worked with his hands as a carpenter, and He experienced the loss of a parent (as His father is not mentioned after His twelfth year). Jesus experienced every aspect of being human, a mere man—and all the suffering that accompanies life in a fallen world.

You need to know Jesus, because to know Him is to experience the full assurance of hope that accompanies His promises, His sacrifices, His high-priestly prayers, and the perfection of His sufferings. There is no moral support that can compare to that of the Son of God made perfect through suffering. Furthermore, if you understand nothing else from this chapter, please try to internalize the staggering love of God's decision to become a created being—forever. He chose to enter into time, limit Himself in space, become dependent upon God as a man, and experience life from a human perspective. As man, God in Jesus Christ will live forever as the servant priest on man's behalf.

Try to internalize the eternal love of God's commitment. His commitment will never end but will go on, and on, and on forever. As stated in Hebrews 7, Jesus did not become a priest for thirty years and then return to heaven to the same state in which He existed before. He became a high priest—forever.

WITHIN GOD IS A
TRANSPARENT HEART

"Then God said, 'Let Us make man in Our image, according to Our likeness.'" (Genesis 1:26)

"But what if God, willing to demonstrate his wrath and to make known his power, has endured with much patience the objects of wrath prepared for destruction? And what if he is willing to make known the wealth of his glory on the objects of mercy that he has prepared beforehand for glory?" (Romans 9:22–23)

Jesus Is Perfectly Just in Punishment and Completely Loving in Forgiveness

CHAPTER 10

JESUS DOES ALL THINGS WELL: THE PERFECTION OF GOD'S LOVE

For Albert Einstein, the answer to the question "Is there a God?" was a simple one. "There has to be a God," he said, "because nothing creates nothing." However, the answer to the question of why there is evil in the world was far more difficult. Albert could not reconcile the Judeo-Christian God of love and justice with all the evil and suffering that exists in the world. And so it is with many today.

Where does evil come from, and why does a holy God permit evil to exist? These are two questions that should not be taken lightly, and a glib answer is certainly not worthy of such a weighty matter. I think most people would agree that until problems surface in our lives we don't give much consideration to finding the answers to the most important questions. For this reason God says in His Word, "It is better to go to a house of mourning than to go to a house of feasting, because that is the end of every man, and the living take it to heart" (Ecclesiastes 7:2). Furthermore, "Sorrow is better than laughter, because sober reflection is good for the heart" (Ecclesiastes 7:3). If there were no problems in our lives, would we care much about the origin of life, how to know God, how we should live, and if is there a judgment to come? Would morality even be an issue if there were no death and suffering in the world?

I can say unequivocally that in this present generation there is far too little faith—even in the existence of God, let alone in a personal and loving God—to consider the meaning of life. People love prosperity preachers who tell them how to have their best life now, but in reality, sorrow is part of everyone's life without exception. A person who goes to church in order to ease his conscience, find comfort for a present sorrow, obtain hope in a present circumstance, or get pumped for a happy life is not seeking truth but something much more selfish. Any preaching that does not change the way people think is not good or biblical. On the one hand, there is the quality of the messenger and his message, and on the other hand is the listener and his motives.

We should first consider seriously whether or not we are seeking truth before we judge whether or not what we hear is the truth. Ask yourself a couple of questions: Do I desire truth for the truth's sake, or do I have an ulterior motive? Am I willing to negotiate the truth for a fantasy to make myself feel better?

Next, it is important to judge whether we have a mind of our own or we have to follow the crowd. The masses are seldom right concerning the really important issues. Ask most people what is important in life, and what will they tell you? The one who ends life with the most toys wins. Eat, drink, and be merry, for tomorrow we die. Education will fix the world. And there is a host of other "truisms" that are anything but true. In reality, the one who ends life with the most toys ends up dead, and death is never a win. The one who eats, drinks, and is merry because he dies tomorrow does not stop to count the cost of eternal judgment. The one who believes that education will fix the world has not considered that in the last and most-educated century, more than 2.3 billion people were murdered.

The masses of men in the West live for today and are not concerned about eternal matters. They deny the existence of the one true God by words and/or works; they are extremely nearsighted when it comes to suffering; and they care not for the truth when it has a cost.

Put aside the thinking of the masses, the lies of false teachers, and the selfish motives of your own heart, and consider the wisdom of the wisest man of all time according to God.

"I have seen all the works which have been done under the sun, and behold, all is vanity [a vapor, a passing breath] and striving after wind" (Ecclesiastes 1:14).

"And I set my mind to know wisdom and to know madness and folly; I realized that this also is striving after wind because in much wisdom there is much grief, and increasing knowledge results in increasing pain" (Ecclesiastes 1:17–18).

"I said to myself, 'Come now, I will test you with pleasure. So enjoy yourself.' And behold, it too was futility" (Ecclesiastes 2:1).

"The wise man's eyes are in his head, but the fool walks in darkness. And yet I know that one fate befalls them both" (Ecclesiastes 2:14).

"So I hated life, for the work which had been done under the sun was grievous to me; because everything is futility and striving after wind" (Ecclesiastes 2:17).

"I know that everything God does will remain forever; there is nothing to add to it and there is nothing to take from it, for God has so worked that men should fear Him" (Ecclesiastes 3:14).

"I have seen that every labor and every skill which is done is the result of rivalry between a man and his neighbor. This too is vanity and striving after wind" (Ecclesiastes 4:4).

"He who loves money will not be satisfied with money, nor he who loves abundance with its income. This too is vanity" (Ecclesiastes 5:10).

All of the previous observations by Solomon have one thing in common: in light of the undeniable truth that all life ends in death, all the ways of man are futile, vain, worthless, and senseless. The man who places all his hopes in this life will without a doubt be disappointed, and he is also called a fool by God: "The fool has said in his heart there is no God." Again, some may say there is a God, but those words are meaningless if the person does not live accordingly.

Therefore, in order to understand the truth—what it is and how it functions—a person must first understand something about himself. We must understand that we are naturally given to fantasy. We avoid the truth because it hurts too much, and we do not wish to look at the reality of death because we do not want to face it. We would rather imagine that we are going to live forever, even though we know that all things die. Only when we face the reality of our own willful ignorance and denial of the truth can we then hope to see the truth. Only when we see the truth will we be able to see God in His glory and above reproach.

God Planned Full Disclosure of Himself

When God set forth to reveal Himself to man, He did not do so by way of tricks, game-playing, or imaginary stories. Everything you read in the Bible is factual, just as everything in life is very real. Death is death, and there is no returning from the grave. God put a plan in motion that would disclose His entire person, but in order to do so, there would have to be full disclosure of both good and evil. We cannot know evil where there is none. Neither can we know compassion, mercy, and forgiveness where there is no need for such divine attributes. Put another way, God could not forgive sin where there was no sin; neither could He judge or punish evil where there was none.

If God were to create a world where evil never manifested itself and required judgment, there would be no way to understand that God is a righteous and holy judge of evil. If God did not have reason to forgive and love people unconditionally, then His ability and willingness to do so could not be known either.

The apostle Paul proclaimed God's plan to fully disclose Himself. "But what if God, willing to demonstrate his wrath and to make known his power, has endured with much patience the objects of wrath prepared for destruction? And what if he is willing to make known the wealth of his glory on the objects of mercy that he has prepared beforehand for glory?" (Romans 9:22–23).

One thing is crystal clear from the previous verses: God's eternal plan is to make Himself known to His creation. From verse 22 we can extract two great realities: (1) God's wrath is toward objects that are prepared for destruction, and (2) the destruction of these objects and God's wrath only occur after He exercises much patience. God exercises patience and withholds wrath, but only for a time. Eventually He employs justice. God cannot tolerate any evil and is naturally inclined to execute speedy vengeance on all who rebel against His perfect and righteous rule. Therefore, it takes great power to restrain His judgment. It takes *great* patience for the one true and holy God to restrain His infinite inclination to exercise righteous judgment upon sin.

Ever since Adam sinned in the garden, God's patience has been clearly seen in the fact that He has been withholding His punishment throughout

136

each person's lifetime. During the first few generations after Adam, men lived for hundreds of years, until God brought total destruction upon the world through a flood, and all were destroyed except for eight people. In the first display of God's coming judgment, He told the world that He would judge sin, which He did through the preaching of Noah for one hundred and twenty years. During the first 1,400 years of man's existence on planet Earth, God exercised great patience toward the evil of men.

"Then the Lord saw that the wickedness of man was great on the earth, and that every intent of the thoughts of his heart was only evil continually. The Lord was sorry that He had made man on the earth, and He was grieved in His heart. The Lord said, 'I will blot out man whom I have created from the face of the land'" (Genesis 6:5).

The first 1,400 years of man's existence proves that without judgment man's sin increases until all that remains is evil. We are told that men's hearts were only evil continually and that his wickedness was great. In the same way, we are told in Ecclesiastes, "Because the sentence against an evil deed is not executed quickly, therefore the hearts of the sons of men among them are given fully to do evil" (Ecclesiastes 8:11).

Notwithstanding, God is revealed as one who is patient. He does not desire that any should perish but that all might come to repentance. However, none of us come to repentance on our own, but we all continue just as we began: enslaved to our own wicked desires, haters of God, and judgmental of others. Throughout the history of the world. men's consciences have told them that they are guilty of wrongdoing, and our judgment of others proves it. Throughout that same time, God has proved Himself to be patient while all men have been evil.

"Therefore you have no excuse, everyone of you who passes judgment, for in that which you judge another, you condemn yourself; for you who judge practice the same things. And we know that the judgment of God rightly falls upon those who practice such things. But do you suppose this, O man, when you pass judgment on those who practice such things and do the same yourself, that you will escape the judgment of God?" (Romans 2:1–3).

God's judgment rightly falls on men who themselves know that what they do is wrong. From Romans 9:22 we see God's wrath and His powerful patience toward instruments of destruction. And another truth is revealed in 9:23: "And what if He is willing to make known the wealth of his glory on the objects of mercy that he has prepared beforehand for glory?" As there are instruments of destruction, so there are instruments of mercy. The former are left as they are: wicked and evil. But the latter are prepared beforehand for glory by the mercy of God. Both instruments, according to Romans 9:21, are taken from the same lump of clay, but one group remains rotten, unformed, useless clay, while the second group is fashioned into a work of art fit for the Master's use. "Or does not the potter have a right over the clay, to make from the same lump one vessel for honorable use and another for common use?" Both groups begin evil, but the latter group becomes righteous by the sacrificial work of the Son of God.

The Reason for Evil in the World

We can answer the question of why there is evil in the world with a simple answer: it exists so God can demonstrate His righteous judgment on evil men, make known His great patience on the same, and make known the wealth of His glory on objects of mercy. All that I have just disclosed is not a game, and it is not done for any temporary period of time but for eternity. These are serious matters, because they involve the time period we refer to as forever. God is serious about these things, and His anger and mercy will have no end. Therefore, since God has revealed Himself in this way, men ought to consider these matters with the utmost sobriety.

God is completely committed in all He does; He is halfhearted in nothing; and He does not make mistake but calculates all His plans to infinite perfection. Why is there evil in the world? Because God does all things well! If God could be satisfied to reveal only part of Himself or to create men in half His image, then there could be only good in the world. But God doesn't work that way. From the beginning God planned to make man in His own complete image. "Then God said, 'Let Us make man in Our image, according to Our likeness'" (Genesis 1:26).

The work of making man in His own image was begun but not finished in the garden of Eden. For that work to be completed, Christ would have to be revealed in all His radiant glory as the sin-bearer and high priest. In real time, the only way to be conformed to the image of

God is to behold His glory, because it is God's glory that creates glory. God tells us this in 2 Corinthians 3:17: "Now the Lord is the Spirit, and where the Spirit of the Lord is, there is liberty. But we all, with unveiled face, beholding as in a mirror the glory of the Lord, are being transformed into the same image from glory to glory, just as from the Lord, the Spirit."

God would have His chosen people walk in the freedom that He walks in: the freedom of righteous living to willingly and willfully choose what is right, with the compulsion that proceeds from a virtuous heart. For this holiness to be created in man—that is, to the extent to which God would create it—there must be evil. Man must behold the complete glory of God, the glory of righteousness as well as the glory of forgiveness, just wrath, compassion, holy indignation, and mercy.

Where we fall short in our thinking is in the fact that we want things easy; wave a wand, cast a spell, and whoosh, it's done. But that's a fairy tale, not reality. The side of God that is willing to suffer for righteousness would go unseen unless there was a reason to suffer. True love is not without a price, and in God there is such a price, not because of evil but in the way the Father loves the Son and gives all glory to Him, and the way the Son loves the Father and gives Him all the glory.

The Holy Spirit, who is equal among the persons of the Trinity, gives all glory to the Father and the Son, and He tells us so in the book He inspired for them both. Man could never know this kind of death apart from the revelation we have in Jesus Christ, His death on the cross, and His eternal intercession as high priest. At the cross there is full disclosure of God's heart, with all His glorious humility, sacrificial love, and holiness.

Think of it: through all eternity, mankind will glory in Christ in such a selfless way that we will all say with every fiber of our being and without any reservation, "I am crucified *[dead]* with Christ, nevertheless I live, yet not I, but Christ lives in me, and the life that I now live in the flesh, I live by faith in the Son of God, who loved me, and gave Himself for me" (Galatians 2:20, emphasis added). It should be very obvious from this verse that such complete self-abandon could only be possible through Christ loving and giving Himself for His chosen people. And it is through the revelation of Himself that men partake in His divine life.

Have you taken part in the divine life of Jesus Christ? If you have, then you have experienced a radical paradigm shift in the direction of your life and faith. Where once you were alienated from God with no loving desire for Him, you now want to know Him better. You desire to please Him, and you have an unselfish longing to live for others. If you have not noticed some change in your desires, longings, and direction, then it may be possible that you have not yet passed from death to life, that you are still outside of the saving work of Jesus Christ. How sad it will be indeed to have learned of the great mysteries of Christ, the love of Jesus, and the sacrifice of the Son of God but never to have appropriated His Word and work for your own. Will you not come to Him today?

You need to know Jesus, because without Him life makes no sense. Even if a person were to get everything he desired, his life would still end in death. No one would want to die if he or she lived in a world where there were absolutely no problems, suffering, sickness, or sadness of any kind. Complete bliss will be the norm in the world that is yet to come. You need to know Jesus because He has a coming kingdom, and He is the only way into that kingdom.

To know Jesus, a person must exercise saving faith in Christ's person and work. Jesus must be received as Lord, which means He is given all the keys to our heart. The Christian does not live a moral life in order to be saved. He lives a moral life *because* he is saved. In order to be saved, you must know Jesus.

WITHIN GOD IS A PATIENT HEART

"He was oppressed and He was afflicted, yet He did not open His mouth; like a lamb that is led to slaughter, and like a sheep that is silent before its shearers, so He did not open His mouth." (Isaiah 53:7)

"And they sang a new song, saying, 'Worthy are You to take the book and to break its seals; for You were slain, and purchased for God with Your blood men from every tribe and tongue and people and nation.'" (Revelation 5:9)

The Most Severe Warning
in the Bible: The Wrath of the Lamb

CHAPTER 11

JESUS'S COMING KINGDOM: THE INTEGRITY OF GOD'S LOVE

When my son was about sixteen years of age, I came in from work and saw him standing in his room just down from our front door. As soon as he saw me, he said, "Dad, come here! I have to show you something."

"What's that?" I asked.

"Read this," he said as he pointed to Revelation 1:4 in his Bible. I began to read the passage aloud. "John to the seven churches that are in Asia: Grace to you and peace, from Him who is—" He stopped me at "who is" and said, "Read it again." Once again I read, "Grace to you and peace, from Him who is—"

He stopped me again and said, "For ten minutes I have been standing here with the thought that *God is*, and I've asked myself, 'Is what?' And all I can think is that *God is.*"

In those moments my son was having a truly worshipful experience with the living God. His heart had been opened by God Himself to acknowledge in a profound way God's existence. It was not purely academic to my son. He was experiencing pure wonder as he contemplated the existence of the one true, self-existent creator of all things.

Before we consider Jesus's coming kingdom, it is important that we have three things properly fixed in our minds so we can properly comprehend this doctrine from the book of Revelation. These three things are vitally important for any person who is to worship God in truth and not in a merely hypocritical and superficial way.

First, such a person must be spiritually renewed, because all men are born to Adam's race spiritually dead, which means that we are deaf, blind, and spiritually ignorant. "But a natural man does not accept the things of the Spirit of God, for they are foolishness to him; and he cannot understand them, because they are spiritually appraised" (1 Corinthians 2:14). Such a renewal is what the Bible refers to as *regeneration* or being *born-again*, and in such a condition a man is made capable of understanding spiritual things.

Second, it is important for a born-again believer to continually humble himself before God so as not to misunderstand what God means by what He has written. Only in proper humility are the regenerate given truth. "Now we have received, not the spirit of the world, but the Spirit who is from God, so that we may know the things freely given to us by God" (1 Corinthians 2:12). Apart from a true, God-given humility, even a born-again believer can be mistaken and/or deceived. "Blessed are the poor in spirit [humble], for theirs is the kingdom of God" (Matthew 5:2).

Third, it is vitally important for regenerate man to rightly interpret God's written Word. The Bible is a book of profound self-revelation of God, so it is a fearful thing to take what He has said and twist it for one's own self-serving purposes. For this reason it is vitally important that the seeker of truth utilize all the rules of proper interpretation so that he may understand what God means by what He has said.

The book of Revelation is no different from any other text in the whole of scripture. Of course, there is imagery in the Bible, just as we use imagery in talking to one another. It is always important to be careful when we seek to understand what someone else says, but we would never think that a letter from a friend was completely metaphorical, symbolic, or allegorical. Yet there are those individuals who want to read every word of Revelation as though it were not at all literal.

Remember that God has written about the most important topics that men will ever contemplate, such as His person and character, requirements and standards for His eternal kingdom, and the means of entering therein, which the Bible calls salvation. We should understand that the greatest communicator in the universe is not unclear about such things.

According to the book of Revelation, Jesus's coming kingdom is the kingdom of the Lamb. He is referred to as "the Lion of the tribe of Judah" two times, as "Jesus" thirteen times, as "Lord" twenty-five times, and "the

Lamb" thirty-two times. The two primary characteristics that God wants us to understand about Jesus through the use of the term *lamb* are (1) His desire for community and (2) His docile, nonaggressive nature.

According to USATODAY.COM, ISTANBUL, Turkey (AP) — First one sheep jumped to its death. Then stunned Turkish shepherds, who had left the herd to graze while they had breakfast, watched as nearly 1,500 others followed, each leaping off the same cliff, Turkish media reported.

According to sheep101.info, there is a certain strain of sheep in Iceland known as leadersheep. Leadersheep are highly intelligent animals that have the ability and instinct to lead a flock home during difficult conditions. They have an exceptional ability to sense danger. There are many stories in Iceland of leadersheep saving many lives during the fall roundups when blizzards threatened shepherds and flocks alike.

It should be obvious from the previous observations about sheep that their survival is dependent upon a good shepherd to lead them. According to chapter 10 of John's gospel, Jesus is the Good Shepherd. "I am the good shepherd," Jesus said. "The good shepherd lays down His life for the sheep" (John 10:11). God desired a people to lead and call His own, a people without rebellion and aggression because of their trust in Him, and for this purpose He laid down His life. People who become God's through faith will have the same desire for community that He has. They will earnestly love, care, and prefer one another and not just look after their own interests (Philippians 2). In a world that has been aflame with unholy anger, that is at war with itself as nation seeks to subjugate nation, that is rampant with murder and mayhem as man rises up against man—in this world Christ has offered Himself as an offering for sin and a means to change the hearts of men from that of a bloodthirsty lion to that of a communal lamb.

We are told that when man sinned he turned away from God, and he did so as an entire race. We are all guilty, and we all carry the same gene for non-communal living. Isaiah, the prophet, put it this way: "All of us like sheep have gone astray, each of us has turned to his own way" (Isaiah 53:6a). In Jesus we see the shepherd of the sheep, but in sinful man we see the sheep that go astray. However, by Jesus's death He brought back the sheep and turned them so they would no longer desire to go astray.

How does Jesus turn sheep so they will only desire to follow Him? For that answer, we look to the docile, nonaggressive nature and character of Christ. We are told in the book of Isaiah, "He was oppressed and He was afflicted, yet He did not open His mouth; like a lamb that is led to slaughter, and like a sheep that is silent before its shearers, so He did not open His mouth" (Isaiah 53:7). The answer to man's waywardness is for Jesus to impart in man His own peaceful, harmless, submissive, unselfish, and loving spirit. Jesus exhibited His lamb-like nature perfectly when He submitted to the Father's will and died upon the cross in man's place.

The End of God's Patience: The Wrath of the Lamb

When at last the day of the Lord's judgment and wrath finally comes, One will be sought among the heavenly inhabitants to release God's restraining hand. At first, none will be found worthy to break the seals, but then the Lion of the tribe of Judah will be recognized as worthy to do so. "And one of the elders said to me, 'Stop weeping; behold, the Lion that is from the tribe of Judah, the Root of David, has overcome so as to open the book and its seven seals'" (Revelation 5:5).

The history of the world is the history of the rise and fall of kingdoms. Men of ambition with a lust for power have sought to conquer people weaker than themselves, which they have accomplished by shedding innocent blood. The Bible, as always, is accurate in its assessment of man: "Their feet are swift to shed blood, destruction and misery are in their paths, and the path of peace they have not known" (Romans 3:15–17).

Only one man in all of history became a conqueror by shedding His own blood. He conquered sin and death, not for selfish reasons but in order to bring true peace to the hearts of men. It is so ironic that the greatest conqueror of all time is referred to in the book of Revelation as the Lamb of God.

"And I saw between the throne [with the four living creatures] and the elders a Lamb standing, as if slain ... And He came and took the book out of the right hand of Him who sat on the throne. When He had taken the book, the four living creatures and the twenty-four elders fell down before the Lamb ... And they sang a new song, saying, 'Worthy are You to take the book and to break its seals; for You were slain, and purchased for God with Your blood men from every tribe and tongue and people and nation'" (Revelation 5:6–9).

At the start of Revelation 5, John begins to weep because no one is found worthy to open the seals, which alone can bring an end to the tribulation of the final days. John's tears are stopped with the pronouncement that the Lion is worthy to open the seals that will bring the final judgments and conflict to earth. Then a twist takes place; it is not the Lion but the Lamb who opens the seals. The Lion of the Tribe of Judah is not mentioned again in the book of Revelation. Only the Lamb executes judgment and brings in the kingdom reign of the Lord Jesus Christ.

The nature of the lion, by God's design, is predatory. It spends part of every day seeking to kill, destroy, and eat the carcasses of other animals. Contrary to the lion, the lamb is always gentle and nonaggressive with all other animals. The lion can be seen to represent God in His righteous anger; He will not leave the guilty unpunished but will destroy the wicked. The lamb, however, represents God's longsuffering, patient, kind, loving nature. In Revelation the wrath of the Lamb is the dominant theme, so it becomes clear that there comes a time when even God's lamb-like forbearance comes to an end.

When God's plan is complete, the Day of His wrath is executed through that part of His nature that is lamb-like. The lion is always ready to pounce, just as God's desire for justice is always present, but as His justice never slumbers, so also His patience and love are equally dominant in His nature. His justice says, in effect, "Punish the guilty," but His forbearance immediately says, "No, we will wait."

There is only one God, but His nature is multifaceted, with complete harmony among all its parts. Because God is completely righteous, He wants to punish evil. But because He is equally patient and loving, He waits for the perfect time. In the book of Revelation, the Lion is replaced by the Lamb to demonstrate for us that God's justice can wait no longer and that His loving patience can endure no more wickedness upon the earth. Final judgment and wrath must fall.

"Then the kings of the earth and the great men and the commanders and the rich and the strong and every slave and free man hid themselves in the caves and among the rocks of the mountains; and they said to the mountains and to the rocks, 'Fall on us and hide us from the presence of Him who sits on the throne, and from the wrath of the Lamb; for the great day of their wrath has come, and who is able to stand?'" (Revelation 6:15–17).

At some point, God will no longer allow Himself to be mocked by men's words, which proceed from their sinful hearts. The knowledge of God's existence has been suppressed in man's unrighteousness (Romans 1). His law, written on the hearts of men though conscience, has been silenced through the hardening of men's hearts (Romans 2:5–6). His law, delivered through Jewish prophets, has been broken (Romans 2:17–24). As a result of this ongoing rebellion, the patience of the Lamb is exhausted, and the final drop of precious love is spent. And so the patience of the Lamb of God is replaced with incomprehensible and eternal rage.

There is a point in history when all that prevents God from executing His justice is removed. We are told in 2 Thessalonians. 2:7, "For the mystery of lawlessness is already at work; only he who now restrains will do so until he is taken out of the way." The phrase "He is taken out of the way" does not appear in the original Greek manuscripts, and while there has been discussion as to what it is that restrains, I believe it is clear that God Himself, in the person of the Lamb, holds back His righteous punishment until the final hour. When the Lamb's patience runs out, all that restrains God's judgment is taken out of the way.

Because of God's fierce anger, the Bible says of us who believe in Him and have been saved by His grace, "Therefore, knowing the fear of the Lord, we persuade men" (2 Corinthians 5:11). We do this because "there is no fear of God before their eyes" (Romans 3:18). People in this unsaved world are in jeopardy every hour of facing God's fierce judgment, and there is no fear of God before their eyes. The Christian walks in the steps of Jesus, who Himself was a hellfire preacher. "But I say to you that everyone who is angry with his brother will be liable to judgment; whoever insults his brother will be liable to the council! And whoever says, 'You fool!' *will be liable to the hell of fire*" (Matthew 5:22, emphasis added).

"And do not fear those who kill the body but cannot kill the soul. Rather *fear Him who can destroy both soul and body in hell!*" (Matthew 10:28, emphasis added).

"If your eye causes you to stumble, throw it out; it is better for you to enter the kingdom of God with one eye, than, having two eyes, to be cast into hell, *where their worm does not die, and the fire is not quenched"* (Mark 9:47–48, emphasis added).

"And you, Capernaum, will not be exalted to heaven, will you? *You will be brought down to Hades!"* (Luke 10:15, emphasis added).

"Now the poor man died and was carried away by the angels to Abraham's bosom; and the rich man also died and was buried. *In Hades he lifted up his eyes,* being in torment, and saw Abraham far away and Lazarus in his bosom. And he cried out and said, 'Father Abraham, have mercy on me, and send Lazarus so that he may dip the tip of his finger in water and cool off my tongue, *for I am in agony in this flame'"* (Luke 16:22–24, emphasis added).

When judgment finally comes upon the earth, the courtroom of God will be in session, the books will be opened, and every evil thing that has ever been said or done will be made known and judged.

"But I tell you that every careless word that people speak, they shall give an accounting for it in the Day of Judgment. For by your words you will be justified, and by your words you will be condemned" (Matthew 12:36–37).

"For the Son of Man is going to come in the glory of His Father with His angels, and *will then repay every man according to his deeds"* (Matthew 16:27).

It will be made perfectly clear in that hour that all men are guilty before God for their trespasses and sins, and at the same time the revelation of God's substitute for sin's penalty will also be revealed: the Lamb of God. All will be punished, but greater condemnation will be upon those who understood the way of salvation (the gospel of Jesus Christ) and rejected it.

"Woe to you, Chorazin! Woe to you, Bethsaida! For if the miracles had been performed in Tyre and Sidon which occurred in you, they would have repented long ago, sitting in sackcloth and ashes. But it will be more tolerable for Tyre and Sidon in the judgment than for you" (Luke 10:13–14).

"Take care not to refuse the one who is speaking! For if they did not escape when they refused the one who warned them on earth, how much less shall we, if we reject the one who warns from heaven?" (Hebrews 12:25).

Israel rejected the law that Moses received from God on Mount Sinai, the law that was meant to inform all men of their guilt. But now men are given the good news of the gospel, wherein we learn that God has given His only begotten Son as an appeasing sacrifice for our sins, and there is a much greater penalty in rejecting the Son. God's greatest wrath will fall upon those who rejected the offer of the Father's love gift. In that hour the Father will give His judgment over to His Son, who will in turn exact justice on all those who rejected the Father's plan and spurned His love.

Within God is a heart for justice, which is centered upon the sacrificial Lamb of God. In the hour of judgment, the all-important question will be: what did we do with Him? Did we love, receive, honor, and obey Him, or did we reject Him?

In the book of Revelation there is a great contrast drawn between the fate of the wicked and the fate of the righteous, the former are judged and thrown into the lake of fire. "Then death and Hades were thrown into the lake of fire. This is the second death, the lake of fire. And if anyone's name was not found written in the book of life, he was thrown into the lake of fire" (Revelation 20:15–16).

The latter are washed and made righteous in the blood of the Lamb, and it is His blood that motivates them to serve and worship Him. As the shepherd, Jesus gave His life for His sheep, and He Himself was a Lamb who proved Himself trustworthy to feed them spiritual truth and give them ample reason to wipe every tear from their eyes.

> I said to him, "My lord, you know." And he said to me, "These are the ones who come out of the great tribulation, and they have washed their robes and made them white in the blood of the Lamb. For this reason, they are before the throne of God; and they serve Him day and night in His temple; and He who sits on the throne will spread His tabernacle over them. They will hunger no longer, nor thirst anymore; nor will the sun beat down on them, nor any heat; for the Lamb in the center of the throne will be their shepherd, and will guide them to springs of the water of life; and God will wipe every tear from their eyes." (Revelation 7:16–17).

The book of Job is probably the oldest account of the devil accusing believers for a lack of obedience to God, implying that God lacks glory for having created such disobedient creatures. "But put forth Your hand now and touch all that he [Job] has; he will surely curse You to Your face" (Job 1:11). In effect, Satan was saying, "Man only serves you because of what you do for him. He does not love you because of who you are, for you are not worthy of love apart from your gifts. At the climax of the Great Tribulation, Satan will be thrown down to hell, and the reason given is that the hour has come for the kingdom of God to replace Satan's rule upon the earth.

"Then I heard a loud voice in heaven, saying, 'Now the salvation, and the power, and the kingdom of our God and the authority of His Christ have come, for the accuser of our brethren has been thrown down, he who accuses them before our God day and night. And they overcame him because of the blood of the Lamb and because of the word of their testimony, and they did not love their life even when faced with death" (Revelation 12:10–11).

Note the phrase "and the kingdom of God and the authority of His Christ have come." The little word *for* explains why: "*for* the accuser of our brethren has been thrown down." At the time God determines to end the devil's rule, He brings in His own, which He does by his own authority and His Christ. It is important to note that the devil's rule has always been within the bounds of what God allows, but on judgment day all authority granted to Satan will come to a complete and final end.

The authority of Christ is in His eternal being, by which He created all things and by which He has all right to reign. However, because man succumbed to the devil's temptations in the garden of Eden, authority over man was given to Satan. The authority to deceive has, throughout all human history, allowed Satan the right to rule by tempting man to sin. Since the first temptation, men have been evil in their hearts, alienated from God, unholy, and unlike Him in character. However, this destructive state has been made much worse by the rule of Satan and his demon army. It is only the blood of the Lamb that sets men free from the power of sin and death and the rule of Satan.

"Therefore, since the children share in flesh and blood, He Himself likewise also partook of the same, that through death He might render powerless him who had the power of death, that is, the devil" (Hebrews 2:14).

The Wrath of the Lamb in Contrast to the Marriage of the Lamb

God in Christ saves His people from His own righteous wrath to come, but just as important is the fact that He saves them from sin itself. "She will bear a Son; and you shall call His name Jesus, for He will save His people from their sins" (Matthew 1:21). In this verse it is not from the wrath of God that men are saved but from sin itself. We are further told in Revelation 14:3 that God's people have a new song in their hearts—the song of praise for their God because He has rescued them from sin itself.

John continued, "These are the ones who have not been defiled with women, for they have kept themselves chaste. These are the ones who follow the Lamb wherever He goes. These have been purchased from among men as first fruits to God and to the Lamb. And no lie was found in their mouth; they are blameless" (Revelation 14:4).

It has been said that we become like that which we worship. If we worship our possessions, we become more materialistic. If we worship ourselves we become more selfish. In the end it will become abundantly clear that men worship the devil, and thereby they have become like him in his hatred and disobedience toward God. But the redeemed have worshipped the Lamb and thereby become like Him. "All who dwell on the earth will worship him [Satan], everyone whose name has not been written from the foundation of the world in the book of life of the Lamb who has been slain" (Revelation 13:8).

As you read these things, I hope you come to a saving knowledge of Jesus Christ. If you have not already, please consider carefully what you worship, and turn from worshipping anything other than the Lamb of God. Worship Him who alone is worthy of worship.

At the end of all false worship is the same fate that will befall the Beast and his image, who are possessed by Satan himself. "He also will drink of the wine of the wrath of God, which is mixed in full strength in the cup of His anger; and he will be tormented with fire and brimstone in the presence of the holy angels and in the presence of the Lamb" (Revelation 14:10).

In contrast to the punishment that is said to come upon the unredeemed and to issue forth from the wrath of the Lamb, there is the marriage ceremony that takes place between the Lamb of God and His bride, a bride made ready by union with Him.

"Hallelujah! For the Lord our God, the Almighty, reigns. Let us rejoice and be glad and give the glory to Him, for the marriage of the Lamb has come and His bride has made herself ready. It was given to her to clothe herself in fine linen, bright and clean; for the fine linen is the righteous acts of the saints" (Revelation 19:6b–8).

Marriage in the economy of God is far more than the joining together of two people who seek pleasure, companionship, and help from each other. It is the actual union of two souls in devotion to one another so deep that it issues forth in a dying to self. Dying to self characterizes the marriage of the Lamb. Therefore, we read that His bride has made herself ready with the righteous acts of the saints. Each and every act of the saints is an expression of their love and devotion to their betrothed. The apex of all devotion is complete death to self through martyrdom, which is also the context of the wedding.

"Hallelujah! Salvation and glory and power belong to our God; because His judgments are true and righteous; for He has judged the great harlot who was corrupting the earth with her immorality, and He has avenged the blood of His slaves on her" (Revelation 19:1–2).

Like a knight in shining armor who comes to the rescue of the fair maiden, the Lamb avenges the blood of His beloved. Those who give their lives for Him are referred to as slaves, for the slave has no rights to his own life but lives completely for the desires of another. Regarding devotion, there is a close similarity between the Master-slave relationship and the marriage of partners who are enveloped by love.

A contrast arises between the metaphor of a knight with a fair maiden and the love of the Lamb for His bride when we realize that the maiden is only made fair through the spilled blood of the Lamb. Apart from the Lamb's blood, the bride was once the enemy. The story that our God tells is one of a far deeper love—unconditional, unselfish, and even incomprehensible. However, the Lamb's love and devotion is so deep and so rich that it places within His bride righteous acts that are deep and rich also. She is adorned with the same love that the Lamb placed upon her, so she becomes a slave until death.

Marriage is a picture by God of the union planned between Himself and His redeemed people. In this union, individuals who were once depraved, rebellious, and evil become conformed to the image of Christ's death (Philippians 3:10, 21). Those who worship the Lamb of God are also recreated in His image, bearing His reproach from a wicked and rebellious world, suffering for His name's sake as they reject the affections, desires, paths, and ways of a wicked and sinful world. A rebellious sinner is always humbled by the thought that God would plan from endless ages past to become one with him, and in so doing share His glory. "Then he said to me, 'Write, "Blessed are those who are invited to the marriage supper of the Lamb."' And he said to me, 'These are true words of God'" (Revelation 19:9).

Make no mistake; it is this union with the Lamb of God that makes the redeemed of the Lord worthy to enter the coming kingdom of God. It is His sacrificial death that removes the curse of death (Galatians 3:13) and turns alienation from God into unity with Him (Ephesians 5:28–32). There is a great truth in the Bible that Christ is in a one-flesh relationship with His people the church. The church is actually referred to as His body in the Ephesians passage I have cited.

God is the only source of all good, and apart from unity with God by faith, men can only be evil. Because of God's love for His people, they willingly serve Him as slaves. "There will no longer be any curse; and the throne of God and of the Lamb will be in it, and His slaves will serve Him" (Revelation 22:3). As created beings, we are always enslaved—either to righteousness through God or to evil through sin, the world, and the devil.

The union of Christ with His people is accomplished by the work of the Holy Spirit. He comes to dwell in the hearts of those who receive Jesus, the Lord, by faith. The testimony that expresses the validity of this union is the transformed lives of the redeemed, which means that they repent of sin (turn from it and cease to live under its absolute control). The redeemed of the Lord (bought by His death) seek with their whole heart (mind, emotions, and will) to serve the Lord Jesus Christ. In the process of being made holy by seeking Him through faith, which the Bible calls *sanctification*, God's children become more like Him in will, desire, and love.

Just prior to my son standing in his room and worshipping God, he had broken up with a girl who had been instrumental in his spiritual growth. Together they'd attended youth group, Bible classes, and all the teaching that the Navigators (a Christian ministry) could produce. After the breakup, my son had spent about three days crying over his loss, and at the end of that time, he began to worship the Lamb that was slain.

A short time later as we were sitting in the kitchen, he said to me, "Dad, I think I know what happened to me recently."

"Really," I said in response.

Then he continued. "All the time I was attending Bible classes, memorizing verses, and listening to lessons prepared to help me see Jesus, I was actually worshipping Susan, and God's Word was not able to penetrate my heart. But when God removed her, He filled me with Himself. It's like a balloon stuck in a water glass. As long as the balloon is in the glass, no water can fill it; it simply flows over the sides. But when the balloon is removed, the water can fill the glass. So when God removed Susan, He filled me with Himself."

Is there anything in your life that is preventing you from receiving Jesus Christ as your Lord? If you cannot be conformed to the image of His death, you will instead be conformed to the thing that you worship. The Jesus who has been pictured for you in the Bible—and by my meager attempts in this book—will be kept from you by the things you worship that are in the world. The choice is yours. However, my hope is that Christ has chosen you, not that you will choose Christ—or so said Charles Spurgeon, and I heartily agree.

You Need to Know Jesus

I once attended a meeting where a missionary friend was sharing at a church about the work that he was doing in New York City among the Jews. One of the questions he received regarded his life in the big city and whether he ever experience fear. He replied, "Perfect love casts out fear, and I know that my Lord loves me perfectly."

There is no substitute for a pure and simple faith in Jesus Christ. The one who receives Christ in truth receives the transforming love of Christ into his heart, and he cannot help but love others also.

"But having the same spirit of faith, according to what is written, 'I believed, therefore I spoke,' we also believe, therefore we also speak, knowing that He who raised the Lord Jesus will raise us also with Jesus and will present us with you" (2 Corinthians 4:13–14).

You need to know Jesus, because a day is coming when the patience of the Lamb will be completely spent. He will cease to restrain the righteous anger of almighty God and instead will call down upon rebellious man all His fiery judgment. You will not want to be among those who have spent their lives mocking God by open rebellion, hypocritical belief, or indifferent agnosticism. In that day it will be too late to repent of sin and believe. The door will be shut, and man will be shut up to all his natural inclinations.

You need to know Jesus, because all who have not received His transforming love will go into eternity as they came into this present life—poor, blind, naked sinners without the one true God. God promises to the believer a new body and soul, which will be shared by God in Christ through the intimacy of the Holy Spirit. There is no such promise to the lost, and they will live forever with the same worn-out body with all the characteristics of the sinner. Fear without confidence will be the state of their condition. Selfishness without generosity, hate without love, and complaint without thankfulness will fill the hearts of those who will be forever tormented among the rest of the damned.

You need to know the Jesus who is God's one and only Son, who alone shares all the divine attributes with His heavenly Father, and who is willing to share them with those who believe in Him.

You need to know that Jesus.

WITHIN GOD IS A HEART OF TRANSCENDENT GLORY

"Who was declared the Son of God with *power* by the resurrection from the dead, according to the Spirit of holiness, Jesus Christ our Lord." (Romans 1:4, emphasis added)

"Now God has not only raised the Lord, but will also raise us up through His *power*." (1 Corinthians 6:14, emphasis added)

"And what is the surpassing greatness of His *power* toward us who believe. These are in accordance with the working of the strength of His might which He brought about in Christ, when He raised Him from the dead and seated Him at His right hand in the heavenly places." (Ephesians 1:19–20, emphasis added)

Jesus lived the life that every man was meant to live, died a death that no other man could die, and was raised from the dead so that men could live through Him.

CHAPTER 12

JESUS'S TRANSCENDENT GLORY: THE TRANSCENDENT GLORY OF GOD'S LOVE

The word *transcend*, according to the *Oxford Dictionary*, means "to be or go beyond the range or limits of something." In the context of this book, we are talking about the character and integrity with which a person lives his or her life. Man is meant for so much more than the way the people of this present world live out their lives. We cannot conceive of all that God has planned for His people in eternity. What we do know is that each person who believes in Jesus Christ for salvation will live with the same characteristics of love and the same integrity of righteousness as God Himself.

God's people will transcend the limits of human achievement, endowed with the very presence of Christ as He lives His life through them. For this reason, I can use words like *purity* and *perfection* when speaking about the life to come. God, who causes something to arise from nothing, will create in man His own moral characteristics with absolute purity to the point of complete perfection.

In this life, however, man is separated from God because of sin until he is reunited with Him through the person and work of His Son, Jesus Christ. The essence of sin is separation *from* God, whereas holiness is separation *unto* God. These two concepts are diametrically opposed to one another.

Human achievement in the world at present is an affront to God.

Man takes all the glory for his accomplishments. There are no monuments or memorials commemorating God's part in scientific, literary, or humanitarian achievements, for God has been stricken from man's consciousness. However, no matter how man denies and ignores God, he cannot escape from God's presence. In fact, man cannot even completely escape from God's standards, because a conscience has been placed within all men by which we judge right from wrong. God's standards can be corrupted and ignored but never completely.

Biblically, man has been made in the image of God, and even though sin has corrupted his heart, he still retains certain aspects of godly character. For this reason, men think themselves to be better than they are. We look at the halls of higher learning, our courts of law, buildings that tower to the sky, and cures in medicine, and we think that we have done something great—as if we could live our lives without divine aid.

Sin is life lived without being conscious of God. Man imagines that he can exist without the Creator. Therefore, no matter what achievements are made in any field, men are destined for destruction because they hate God, and they reveal their hatred by ignoring His ongoing activity to sustain their existence (Romans 1:18–23).

In contrast to sinfully wicked men—who by their behavior deny the existence of God—is the God/man, Jesus Christ. He existed eternally with the Father in perfect and limitless harmony and love, and by Him God saves those who believe.

Jesus Lived the Life That Every Man Was Meant to Live

Before the creative act of God, there was the expression of God as recorded in John's first letter. "What was from the beginning, what we have heard, what we have seen with our eyes, what we have looked at and touched with our hands, concerning the Word of Life—and the life was manifested, and we have seen and testify and proclaim to you the eternal life, which was with the Father and was manifested to us—" (1 John 1:1–2).

The expression of God is the Lord Jesus Christ. He was sent into the world to save men from the penalty of their sin, and by so doing to reveal the character of the eternal God. As the above verse tells us, Jesus "was" from the beginning. Before all created things began, He already was.

The apostles were privileged to witness God in human flesh. They heard Him speak, saw Him act, and touched the physical form that had been prepared for Him. He is the Word of life, the life, and the eternal life that was with the Father. The second person of the triune God became human in Jesus Christ. It is this Jesus who fulfilled the Father's plan to live life as every man was meant to live it.

The old expression, "if you want something done right, you have to do it yourself" describes exactly what God did in Christ. The life that Jesus lived as a man during His thirty-three years on earth was completely consistent with His existence throughout eternity. He lived in unbroken communion with the Father and the Holy Spirit. It is this type of union with God that is reserved for those of us who are saved by His grace. "And you were dead in your trespasses and sins" (Ephesians 2:1). "Because of His great love with which He loved us, even when we were dead in our transgressions, made us alive together with Christ" (Ephesians 2:4–5). The union that the believer has with God in Christ would be unattainable apart from the incarnation of Jesus Christ and the life He lived out as the God/man.

Through Jesus's existence as a man, He identified with men so they could be freed from the penalty of their sin through Jesus's death. Through identification with Jesus in His resurrection, men who are dead in trespasses and sins are raised from the dead and made righteous in God's sight. Sanctification is the process by which Jesus takes the man made right with God by identification with Him and makes him righteous in word and deed by imparting in his heart God's holy law (Hebrews 10). The first is instantaneous, and the second takes place over time in this life—or instantly at the believer's death or Jesus's return.

Jesus's union with the Father is at the core of the Father's plan for saved men. The Father and the Son have an imperishable union based on mutual love and honor. Within their union they share the same thoughts, desires, will, emotions, and characteristics. These are imparted to the believer after salvation.

"Therefore Jesus answered and was saying to them, 'Truly, truly, I say to you, the Son can do nothing of Himself, unless it is something *He sees the Father doing*; for whatever the Father does, these things the Son also does in like manner. For the Father loves the Son, *and shows Him all things that He Himself is doing*" (John 5:19–20, emphasis added).

The Father shows the Son all things that He Himself is doing, because they exist in perfect harmony. They know each other's thoughts perfectly and completely. The Father hides nothing from the Son, as the Son hides nothing from the Father. Man, of course, will never be able to comprehend the infinite God, but the oneness that the Father and Son share will become the believer's experience as the Son lives out His life through man.

The 1924 Olympic gold medalist Eric Liddell was a missionary to China for the majority of his life until his death in a Japanese civilian internment camp in 1945. His life goal was best articulated by writer Colin Welland (*Chariots of Fire*) when he put into Eric's mouth these words: "I believe that God made me for a purpose. But He also made me fast, and when I run, I feel His pleasure."

To feel the pleasure of God is the greatest satisfaction any created being can have, and it is the greatest fulfillment of one's existence. To feel God's pleasure is to be of one mind with Him. Sinful, carnal man cannot value or appreciate such a pleasure. It is the pleasure of God that believers feel best when they appropriate the law of God that is placed in their hearts through identification with Jesus Christ.

However, there is a great contrast between Jesus Christ and the rest of humanity. Christ is one with God the Father in ways that the rest of mankind does not even care to know about. Christ is diametrically opposed to the direction humanity is headed, the purpose that drives men, the motives that activate them, and the mind-sets that direct them. Christ is part of the divine Trinity, which in and of itself is incomprehensible to mere men, but the elect know that it is true because it is found in God's infallible Word.

The Trinity is three distinct persons in one God. It is Jesus's character within the context of the perfect union of the divine Trinity that we are contemplating in this part of the chapter. This union within God defines the pure perfection of Jesus, and separation from God defines the sinfulness of wicked mankind. Jesus Christ is the one and only man by whom believing sinners can enter into a union with the living God.

The means of God's grace to reveal God the Father to sinners is the work of Jesus Christ. Only Jesus can reveal the Father, because He alone knows Him. "All things have been handed over to Me by My Father; and no one knows the Son except the Father; nor does anyone know the Father except the Son, and anyone to whom the Son wills to reveal Him" (Matthew 11:27).

It is this knowledge of God that separates saved and obedient saints from damned and disobedient sinners. The good works that all men do are not the measuring line for salvation. Salvation is accomplished through works accomplished by, through, and for the glory of God through our Lord Jesus Christ. The transforming work that Christ accomplishes in the saint is accomplished through man's accurate knowledge of Christ, which is why Jesus defined eternal life in the following way: "This is eternal life, that they may *know You*, the only true God, and Jesus Christ whom You have sent" (John 17:3, emphasis added).

There is knowledge about Jesus that actually hardens the heart of the sinner, but there is also knowledge of Jesus that transforms the heart of the saint. The same sun that hardens the clay melts the wax. The true knowledge of Jesus is the same with regard to the basic facts, but to one person the knowledge may become intensely personal, applicable, and transforming. To another person it may be tragically rejected.

Communication with Jesus Is the Pathway to God

In His humanity, the Son of God learned what it is to pray as a man. It sounds surreal to say that God learned something, because He knows all things. However, in this truth we come to understand the humility of Jesus Christ. The infinite God does not know weakness experientially anymore than He knows evil, but in the creation plan He humbled Himself to experience weakness. Jesus became hungry, thirsty, and tired. In the same way, Jesus prayed as men pray. At the time when Jesus chose twelve men to be with Him, He prayed all night. "It was at this time that He went off to the mountain to pray, and He spent the whole night in prayer to God" (Luke 6:12).

Jesus entered fully into the experience of being a man, and when He prayed, He prayed not only as the Son of God but as one who was fully human. Jesus prayed the way every man was meant to pray; He prayed in perfect and unbroken union with His Father. It cannot be repeated enough that the most distinguishing and defining mark of the way Jesus lived a life acceptable to His heavenly Father—unlike the way men are rejected by God—was His intimate union with God. The intimacy that Jesus shares and enjoys as the God/man with His Father is shared with those He calls to Himself through a true knowledge of Him.

The greatest spiritual awakening in history since that founding of the church by Jesus through the apostles was the Great Awakening, which took place largely in England and America. It began in England in the 1930s, and its effects are still felt today in many ways. At the forefront of this act of God that brought salvation to many thousands of people was a man by the name of Howell Harris. Educated in Wales and reared in a prominent family, he went the way of wicked men after the death of his father. However, God came down upon him in a mighty way, took hold of his soul, and transformed him into a repentant sinner.

Harris's passion for Christ and the souls of lost men became so great that he was received by masses of people in the open air, because the religious elite rejected his saving message of Christ for damned sinners. He faced much in the way of persecution by religious and nonreligious alike, but his fervor could not be quenched. Jesus told His disciples, "If the world hates you, it hated Me first" (John 15:18). Howell, however, was given an amazing prayer life by which his communion with God became very great, and one man with God can accomplish much.

Harris's wonderful zeal for Jesus all began with a vibrant prayer life. When speaking about it in *George Whitefield* Volume 1 (pg. 239), Arnold Dallimore wrote this:

> Harris's knowledge of Divine things during these days was small. He simply knew he loved the Lord and wanted to love Him more, and in this pursuit he sought out quiet places where he could be secluded with Him in prayer. One of his favorite retreats was the church at Llangasty village … and on one occasion shortly after his conversion he climbed into its tower to be the more alone with the Lord. There, as he remained in intercession for some

hours, he experienced an overwhelming sense of the presence and power of God. That lonely church tower became to him a holy of holies, and he afterwards wrote, "I felt suddenly my heart melting with me, like wax before the fire, with love to God my Savior; and also felt, not only love and peace, but a longing to be dissolved and be with Christ. There was a cry in my inmost soul which I was totally unacquainted with before, 'Abba Father!' ... I knew that I was His child, and that He loved and heard me. My soul being filled and satiated, cried, 'It is enough! I am satisfied! Give me strength and I will follow Thee through fire and water!'" This was indeed a hallowed experience to Harris. It proved to be a mighty infilling of the Holy Spirit, empowering him for the ministry of incessant labors, violent opposition and spiritual victories which lay directly before him. (*George Whitefield*

What became a whirlwind experience with God for Howell Harris is meant for every believer, even though personal ministry can vary greatly. I would love to disclose Jesus to my readers in such a meaningful way that they could all know Him well enough to become saved and grow to total maturity in Him.

However, that is impossible. Growing into maturity, like receiving Christ for salvation, is something that must be experienced. It comes through a knowledge of the truth, but it must be much more than a mere intellectual awareness of some select facts. Many single people have learned a great deal about marriage from family and friends, but there is a world of difference between knowing about marriage and being married. Relationships are the most complicated experience in life, and a person must be fully committed to a relationship to experience good fruit from it.

Faith in Jesus's Equality with God Is the Pathway to Life

All cults have in common a denial of the divinity of Jesus Christ. They may say that He is the Son of God, a messenger, a prophet, or a great teacher of God, but they all deny the biblical reality that Christ is God in the flesh.

To know Jesus, you have to receive Him for who He is and not who you want Him to be. The true Christian is the person who talks to God and accepts Jesus's teaching that He is one with God the Father.

Only God can give life, as He is the source of life. Therefore, Jesus's words become undeniable: He is the second person of the Trinity, and as such, He gives life. "For just as the Father raises the dead and gives them life, even so the Son also gives life to whom He wishes" (John 5:21).

Honor and glory belongs to God alone. When men receive honor correctly, it is understood that it is by the grace of God, which means that God ultimately gets the glory for working through men. Men are merely the vessels through whom God works, and it is the grace of God that allows men to receive honor for what God is doing. However, Jesus does not speak of Himself in such a way. Jesus does not receive honor because God works through Him; He receives His own honor.

If you would be intimate with God and share your heart with Him, you must speak to God through His Son. The work that God does, He always does through His Son, and He only listens to men who speak through His Son. Think on Jesus's words: "But He answered them, 'My Father is working until now, and I Myself am working'" (John 5:17). He did not say that God was working through Him, or that He worked by the grace of God, which was what the apostle Paul said. Rather, Jesus said, "And I Myself am working."

Even the religious leaders of Jesus's day realized that Jesus revealed Himself to be equal with God. "For this reason therefore the Jews were seeking all the more to kill Him, because He not only was breaking the Sabbath, but also was calling God His own Father, making Himself equal with God" (John 5:18).

Jesus never broke the sabbath, but He is Lord of the sabbath. On the seventh day of creation, God rested (Genesis 2), which means that He stopped to appreciate the work of His own hands. The sabbath day of rest was given to men for that very same reason: to enter into honoring God for His glorious work of creation (Exodus 20:8–11). Jesus is the end of the work of the law for all those who believe (Romans 10:4). Therefore, He is the sabbath rest.

Jesus purposely healed the sick on the sabbath for three reasons: (1) the works He performed were authentication that He was the long-awaited

Savior and God (John 14:11; Matthew 1:23); (2) He had compassion on those who suffered because of illness (Matthew 14:14); and (3) as God, Jesus's healing on the sabbath was not taking away from God the honor that was due His name, but rather He gave God honor for His compassion and power to heal.

The Jews sought Jesus's death because He made Himself equal with God. Do you bow to Jesus as Lord and God, or would you rather seek His death because He makes Himself equal with God?

Jesus is God in human flesh, and for this reason He died a death that no other man could die.

Jesus Died the Death That No Other Man Could Die

Nowhere do we get a clearer glimpse into the soul of Christ concerning the trauma He felt in anticipation of the cross than when He prayed in the garden of Gethsemane. The Bible does not give the details of Christ's suffering, because crucifixion was well known to the Jews—and because the physical suffering paled by comparison to what Jesus suffered from God. The Bible only records that Jesus was crucified.

Let us consider carefully Jesus's agony during the hours He spent in the garden. "And He went a little beyond them, and fell on His face and prayed, saying, 'My Father, if it is possible, let this cup pass from Me; yet not as I will, but as You will.' And He came to the disciples and found them sleeping, and said to Peter, 'So, you men could not keep watch with Me for one hour? Keep watching and praying that you may not enter into temptation; the spirit is willing, but the flesh is weak'" (Matthew 26:39–40).

If you have ever been broken by the circumstances of life or have ever felt worthless, guilty, helpless, depressed, or just deeply sorrowful, you know that the floor is a very appropriate place to be. Jesus fell on His face when He prayed. It was not merely an act of humility for Him, but it went to the depths of His soul as He began to be separated from the Father's loving and tender care.

For thirty-three years He experienced the humility of being human. He denied His divine attributes of omniscience, omnipresence, and omnipotence. He relinquished His divine attributes to the Holy Spirit for miraculous acts of healing—as when He raised Lazarus from the dead—in order to identify with men who must rely upon God for everything. His identification with humanity demanded His dependence upon God. He never ceased to be God, even though in His great humility He relied upon God the Father and the Holy Spirit. However, Gethsemane took humility and suffering to a whole new level for Jesus.

In the garden Jesus prayed, "My Father," which was not uncommon for Him, but on this very difficult night it had a special significance. Every fiber of His being was focused on the paramount reality that He was about to be separated from His Father's approval. In eternity, Jesus had never known separation from the Father. No other man could have died the death that Jesus did, because no sinner would suffer as a result of separation from God as Jesus did. The only people who suffer separation from God are those who have idolatrous love and worship for a false god.

We are a generation of people who have suffered under the loss of parental love, if by nothing more than separation from our parents. Broken homes have produced broken hearts among so many children. Selfishness has replaced self-sacrifice on the part of parents, and the end result is hurt people who have suffered for lack of a father's or mother's nearness. In this way we can understand to a small degree what Jesus experienced in being separated from the one He loved most dearly and infinitely.

Often children feel the loss of approval from parents by separation from them, whether the parent disapproves of them or not. In contrast to the devastating effect that parental neglect has had on people in the American experience of the twentieth century, the Godhead has experienced perfect and unending love and honor in an eternal state. It is no wonder that Jesus sweat great drops of blood as He contemplated receiving the Father's disapproval as He became sin in man's place. "My Father, if it is possible, let this cup pass from Me."

Desperation is not a characteristic of God, so it was in humiliation that the Son of God asked, "My Father, if it is possible"—meaning, if it was within God's power. This does not sound like the same Jesus who said, "With people this is impossible, but with God all things are possible" (Matthew 19:26). Did Jesus think something could be outside of the

Father's power? We can be assured that Jesus did not question the Father's abilities.

It would appear that Jesus spoke out of desperation. He was facing a trial beyond human imagination. The infinite Son of the Father's love allowed Himself to be torn from the Father's approval. It was as if He said, "You are the all-powerful One, the One who is able to rise above circumstances. Therefore, if there is any other way, let this cup pass from me."

Jesus knew in the depths of His soul that there was no other way. Had there been another way, the Father surely would not have sent His Son to judgment. What Jesus spoke to the Father, He spoke from His heart, from the very depths of His being. He did not shrink back from the Father's will or even His own. He spoke from His revulsion over being identified with sin.

Jesus felt in His heart the full weight of the Father's abhorrence of sin because, being God, He felt it also. Therefore He said, "Yet not as I will, but as You will." Out of love for the Father, He was willing to receive hate from the Father as He stood in the sinner's place. Ultimately, He knew that the Father would exalt Him to a place of no other, that the Father's approval would be restored. But first the cross would have to be experienced so that the Father's will could be honored.

Jesus desired for the cup to pass. Not just any cup but *this* cup. It was the cup of judgment that Jesus disdained (Hebrews 12:2). The prophet Habakkuk spoke about the cup of judgment in regard to God's coming judgment upon Babylon. "You will be filled with *disgrace* rather than honor. Now you yourself drink and expose your own *nakedness*. The *cup* in the LORD'S *right hand* will come around to you, and utter *disgrace* will come upon your *glory*" (Habakkuk 2:16).

At the cross it would not be Babylon that would experience the cup of God's wrath but Jesus, His Son. The Lord's right hand, or the hand of His power, would be brought down upon the back of His beloved Son. Disgrace, not honor, awaited Jesus as He lay upon the ground in Gethsemane. The nakedness of sin's disgrace would be His covering, not the glory of His eternal goodness.

However, the words still rang out from His lips at least two more times in the garden: "Yet not as I will, but as You will." Jesus laid aside His divine right to choose and His divine preference to receive the Father's approval, because He loved the Father. Lest you think the Father is some kind of monster for requiring such suffering from His Son, know that the Father endured all the same torment when He punished the Son as He stood in man's place. God's ways are not our ways; He does all things right.

No man has ever been one with God the Father in the eternal state. No man is infinitely sinless, perfectly pure, and completely holy. No man can take the righteous punishment for all the sins of all the people in every age in all the world upon himself, and suffer to God's satisfaction. It is ludicrous to think otherwise, unless you think man to be equal with God. Jesus died a death that no other man could die so that when He rose from the dead, men might live as God intended through Him.

Jesus Was Raised from the Dead So That Men Could Live through Him

The Christianity of Christ is nothing like the Christianity of the world. When facing persecution from the false system of Judaism, and confronted by the Roman ruler Pilate, Jesus said, "My Kingdom is not of this world" (John 18:36). Jesus was resurrected back to life so that men might live as God intended through Him.

Christianity as Christ intended it is life lived as Christ lived it. It is the eternal life of Christ flowing through the soul of the believer who has been raised from the dead. "When you were dead in your transgressions and the uncircumcision of your flesh [a person not separated to God for His purpose and glory], He made you alive together with Him, having forgiven us all our transgressions" (Colossians 2:13).

When Jesus raised Lazarus from the dead, He turned to Martha, Lazarus's sister, and said to her, "Did I not say to you that if you believe, you will see the glory of God?" (John 11:40). Jesus is glorified in the resurrection of His people. Resurrection is not simply about the body; it is a new direction, desire, goal, purpose, and motive in the life of the soul. The resurrection in Christian terms is the resurrected life of Christ lived out in the minds and hearts of His people.

After World War II, a few bombers that had been used for missions of destruction were taken over for commercial service. They were called converted bombers. The converted bombers had new owners. They carried new cargo. They had new pilots. In the new birth (Matthew 19:28; Titus 3:5), the soul of the penitent sinner is converted by the infusion of the life of Christ. The person remains, but he is transformed from sinner to saint, and at the final resurrection he is made perfect and sinless.

Christ is at the head of the resurrected believer, where He belongs, and all that the saint desires is according to the law of the Lord. He serves Christ from his heart, which means he is not coerced but made new. He functions as he was intended, no longer corrupted by selfish desires and goals but for God's glory and the well-being of others. Selfishness is turned into selflessness by the presence of Christ. The characteristics that are present in the Christ and seen through the Gospels are made to work in the heart of those who repent and believe.

The words that were true of Paul as Christ lived out His life in him are true of every Christian, according to the power that works within him. "I am crucified with Christ, nevertheless I live, yet not I but Christ lives in me, and the life that I now live in the flesh, I live by faith in the Son of God, who loved me and gave Himself for me" (Galatians 2:20).

There is no eternal life apart from a resurrection from the dead. No salvation! No joy! No peace! "The wicked are like the troubled sea when it cannot rest," said the prophet Isaiah (Isaiah 57:20). Christianity is the conversion of the wicked so that they begin to take on the characteristics of Christ through His Spirit that abides within. Resurrection is just that: it is the sinner raised from the dead so that old things pass away and all things become new in time and eternity, as stated in 2 Corinthians 5:17.

False religion is a pretentious worship of a false god, which denies the power of the true God (2 Timothy 3:5). True Christianity is the display of God's power through the transformation of sinners. It places on display the attributes of Christ, which are revealed in the Gospels and carried out through the lives of His saints. The New Testament saint is not a stained-glass figure meant to be worshipped in place of Christ, as false converts give credit to the saint rather than the Savior. The New Testament saint is a sinner bought by the blood of Christ, forgiven, cleansed, and made new. He or she is not a person to be admired but a channel through whom God is glorified.

False converts are self-deceived, thinking themselves to be something they are not because they have never repented of sin and believed in Christ as God requires. The resurrection from the dead is not something a man can accomplish by his own power. A dead person cannot stand up and walk. The dead do not talk at their own funerals. The cruelty of death to the parent who has lost a child or a child who has lost a parent is in the finality of it.

In resurrection the finality of death is broken, and life is once again realized. In true Christianity there is no self-deception, no false repentance and belief, and no finality of death. The repentance is real because Christ lives. He lives in the heart of the believer, and therefore the relationship is restored. False converts try to live out their faith under their own power, but the true Christian is the work of the resurrected Christ. The New Testament saint is one of the dead brought back to life. He is a new self who is being renewed according to the image of the One who created him—even Christ (Colossians 3:10).

Some professing themselves to be Christian attempt to work their way to heaven while all the while denying Christ, howbeit so subtly at times that they may be mistaken for the real thing. They attempt by good works to enter the kingdom of heaven. The apostle Paul was amazed at how quickly the people at Galatia deserted the one who called them by the grace of Christ for another gospel (Galatians 1:6). They had turned the gospel of grace into a gospel of works, which is no gospel (good news) at all.

Those who experience resurrection of life come to understand the gospel in truth. God saves sinners because they cannot save themselves; and if they could save themselves, then Christ would have suffered and died needlessly. Therefore, the good works that God produces in His people are not to merit heaven, for God has made them worthy of heaven through the finished work of Christ and not through merit in their own sinful strivings.

Other false Christians set themselves "free" to commit every form of sin, because they believe themselves to be saved when in fact they do not know Christ. Such a fake freedom is another form of bondage whereby the sinner becomes enslaved to another lie of the devil. The resurrection of Christ sets men free from the guilt of sin and a defiled conscience, and it works righteousness. But it also sets converts on a path to obey Christ rather than to justify their old manner of life (Colossians 2:13; 3:5–6).

A Final Plea for Your Soul

If you have never come to a saving knowledge of Jesus Christ, you need to. The Jesus of the Bible is the Jesus you need to know, because apart from that Jesus it is impossible to know divine character in truth. The culmination of a life without God, no matter how rewarding it may appear to be, is empty of godly righteousness and filled with fear and false hope.

The only solution for a life lived in futility and striving after the wind (Ecclesiastes 1:14) is to know Jesus Christ. Apart from Christ, your sins will vastly outweigh any good you think you have done to merit heaven. If you appear before God and argue your case to enter heaven, not having come to a saving knowledge of Christ in truth, you will bring upon yourself the wrath of the Father for having trampled underfoot His Son's sacrifice and insulted the Spirit of grace by which you think you are saved (Hebrews 10:29).

Jesus is the only servant who is worthy of honor before almighty God, which means that the only way to receive honor for service before God is to be found in Him. Jesus, having become a man, is the only leader who is worthy to produce true servitude in His followers. Jesus alone has proven Himself a worthy leader, because He alone serves mankind with absolutely nothing to gain from His creation except that which He Himself imparts. Jesus offered a worthy submission to God through thirty years of submission to His earthly mother and stepfather.

Apart from knowing Jesus and being found in Him, there is no acceptable submission that a sinner can offer to God. Every man born to a woman in Adam's race is guilty of sin and worthy of eternal punishment, and to deny the same is to reveal the sin that lies within all our hearts. Jesus alone is a worthy comforter to all sinners who make their refuge in Him.

Jesus defined His love for sinners while standing on a hill outside of Jerusalem, praying to His Father and interceding for His followers. There is no greater love than that of Christ, who alone stands in the gap between a holy God and sinful men.

You need to know Jesus, because His sacrifice alone is acceptable to the Father. Any sacrifice you think worthy before God that has not come through the sacrifice of His Son will bring you greater condemnation than you can possibly imagine. You need to know Jesus.

Jesus defines unity as it is displayed in marriage, and it will be displayed between Him and His bride, the church, forever. Apart from Jesus you will never know unity with God, and that is a unity that you definitely should want to know. Jesus is a faithful high priest. He will bring His brethren continually before God and make them acceptable worshippers through His Spirit that dwells within them throughout eternity.

Jesus instituted the perfect plan because He does all things well. He can be trusted because He is a God of love in every conceivable way to men—and every way they cannot conceive of.

Jesus is not someone you want to face when He returns to earth to exercise wrath when His patience as the Lamb of God is exhausted. He has proven Himself to be patient for thousands of years as He has waited for sinners to repent and come to Him for forgiveness, cleansing, and resurrection life. When His patience comes to an end, it will be finished forever.

You need to know Jesus before your earthly life is over, and you don't know when that moment will come. For that reason, you need to know Jesus *now*. Jesus is transcendent in glory, and if for no other reason, you should want to know Him because He is worthy of praise.

If you have never come to a saving knowledge of Jesus Christ, will you come to Him today?

Printed in the United States
By Bookmasters